"Not only is this book full of provocative answers that college students need to hear, it's full of the tough, real-life questions that college students are looking to ask and we are many times afraid to hear. I value Professor Theophilus's biblical wisdom he shares with students, but more importantly I appreciate the relationships he has built with college students and his willingness to truly listen to them. I wish I had a book and professor like this when I was in college."

—MARK L. EARLEY
president, Prison Fellowship

"Discover over and over God's sensible perspectives as you eavesdrop on Theophilus dialoguing with those who question or challenge him on issues of behavior and belief. Learn not only biblically sound, logically consistent content but also the techniques of firm, loving engagement, and become a more skillful ambassador in the process."

—DAVID C. NESS
PhD, university faculty ministry consultant

"The very best advice column available for young Christians is that written by the ever wise and always witty Professor Theophilus. Reading the good professor's latest book, *Ask Me Anything 2*, one wonders if the Lord hasn't suddenly made the wisdom of Solomon available to us again while insisting that his wisdom be delivered with just a dab of flair and charm. Buy this book for all the young Christians you know and they'll not only gain invaluable perspective, insights, and solutions to many of the problems already confronting them, they'll also learn how to think about problems in general as faithful believing Christians should."

—J. FRASER FIELD
executive officer, The Catholic Educator's Resource Center

"Professor Theophilus is great. He is wise, penetrating, and always right on target. This book offers spiritual guidance that college students will take in like pizza. Even this old retired professor couldn't put it down and learned a lot."

—PHILLIP E. JOHNSON
professor of law emeritus, University of California, Berkeley,
author of Darwin On Trial

"It is one thing to read about natural law in *What We Can't Not Know*, but it is quite another to have J. Budziszewski (aka Professor Theophilus) show you how to apply it in real-life situations. Students and adults will learn so much about how to apply reason and biblical truth to their everyday world in *Ask Me Anything* 2. It's a great resource you need to read."

—KERBY ANDERSON
national director for, Probe Ministries; host, Point of View *radio talk show*

"J. Budziszewski is one of the most gifted thinkers and writers in the Christian world today, a winsome example of how one ought to answer difficult questions about the faith with clarity, charity, and real insight. As the redoubtable, though accessible, Professor Theophilus, Budziszewski offers to his questioners the deep resources of the Christian faith in such a way that his answers illuminate dark patches of ignorance the present age presents as wisdom. Every Christian attending or planning to go to college (or, dare I say, teaching college!) should master the style and substance of both this book and its predecessor."

—FRANCIS J. BECKWITH
associate professor of philosophy and church-state studies, Baylor University

ASK ME ANYTHING

more provocative answers for college students

2

j. budziszewski
(aka professor theophilus)

© 2008 by J. Budziszewski

ISBN-10: 1-60006-193-1
ISBN-13: 978-1-60006-193-6

Cover design by Disciple Design
Cover illustration Getty Images

Unless otherwise identified, all Scripture quotations in this publication are taken from the *Revised Standard Version Bible* (RSV), copyright 1946, 1952, 1971, by the Division of Christian Education of the National Council of the Churches of Christ in the USA, used by permission, all rights reserved.

Library of Congress Cataloging-in-Publication Data

Budziszewski, J., 1952-
  Ask me anything 2 / J. Budziszewski. -- 1st ed.
    p. cm.
  Sequel to: Ask me anything.
  Includes bibliographical references and index.
  ISBN-13: 978-1-60006-193-6 (alk. paper)
  ISBN-10: 1-60006-193-1 (alk. paper)
  1. Christian college students--Religious life. 2. Christian college
students--Conduct of life. I. Title. II. Title: Ask me anything two.
BV4531.3.B825 2008
248.8'34--dc22
                                    2008001645

Printed in the United States of America

1 2 3 4 5 6 7 8 9 10 / 12 11 10 09 08

CONTENTS

FLEEING FROM GOD STUFF

FLEEING TOWARD GOD STUFF

ACKNOWLEDGMENTS

Thanks are due chiefly to Sandra, crown of my home and light of my eyes.

Acknowledgment is also due to Alexandra, for patient answers to many odd questions about pop culture and dialect;

To Arlen Nydam and Ben Hicks, for confirming the inscription at the library;

To everyone who wrote to Theophilus;

To everyone who told me that he had made a difference in their lives;

And to all my students, known and unknown. May the Father of Lights illuminate the paths of their studies.

INTRODUCTION

IN MY FORMER BOOK, THEOPHILUS . . .

Acts 1:1

I hope you enjoy this second volume of the conversational adventures of Professor M. E. Theophilus, holder of the PMS Chair[1] in the School of Antinomianism at Post Everything University. In case you were wondering, he is not the same as the biblical Theophilus to whom St. Luke wrote the Gospel of Luke and the Acts of the Apostles, although he was named after him. That also explains his initials.[2]

Ask Me Anything 2 isn't just more of the same. It includes not just new material, but new kinds of material. You'll see that reflected in the letters, too. I explain some of the differences in the introductions to each of the four sections.

Sometimes people wonder what sort of place Post Everything University is. Frankly, it's not much different than most universities these days. At the east end of the main quad is the great iron gate of the Dis Memorial Library, each side of its rusty arch declaring half of the school's Latin motto — on one side, for those going in, *Non Cognoscetis Veritatem*, "you shall not know the truth," and on the other, for those coming out, *Et Dubitatio Liberabit Vos*, "and doubt shall set you free." That pretty well sums up the school's creed. Not many people know that when the school was founded, the motto on the gate was different: *Cognoscetis Veritatem, Et Veritas Liberabit Vos*, "You shall know the truth, and the truth shall set you free." These words were said by Christ to His disciples. They still sum up Theophilus' creed. Mine too.

Ever since I began writing about him, people keep introducing me as "Professor Theophilus." Allow me to take this opportunity to declare that we are not the same person; I am merely his friend and chronicler. Even my editors confuse us. I'll bet the cover of this book will say "aka Professor Theophilus" underneath my name. A bio line in one of my online columns about Theophilus[3] misleadingly declared that "J. Budziszewski drinks his coffee black, strong and bitter." No, that's how he drinks it. I, of course, use cream. I hope this settles the controversy.

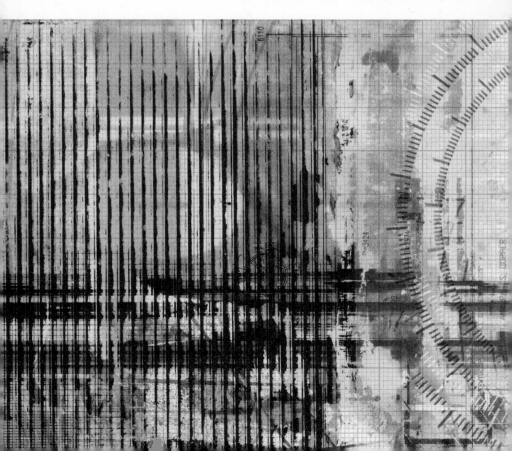

LEARNING TO THINK STUFF

CHAPTER ONE

WHAT THIS SECTION IS ABOUT

I wrote in the introduction that *Ask Me Anything 2* includes not just new material, but new kinds of material. The differences start right here. *Ask Me Anything 1* included a section called "Faith on Campus Stuff". Though I still like what I put in it, that title gave the impression that some things on campus are related to faith and others aren't. Actually that's not true; everything is related to faith.

The reason you're on campus, though, is chiefly to learn how to think. You're there to learn other things too — like the wisdom traditions of your civilization and the things you need to know for your future profession — but learning to think comes first.

Thinking means reasoning, not feeling. It also means thinking *faithfully*. As a great Christian of our time has written, "Faith and reason are like two wings on which the human spirit rises to the contemplation of truth; and God has placed in the human heart a desire to know the truth — in a word, to know himself — so that, by knowing and loving God, men and women may also come to the fullness of truth about themselves."[4]

Some of your professors may disagree, so "Learning to Think Stuff" talks about that problem too.

CHAPTER TWO

I FEEL LIKE, THEREFORE I AM

THINK WITH YOUR FEELINGS, FEEL WITH YOUR—NO, WAIT—

Once again, the lock on my office door wasn't cooperating with the key. I felt like a safecracker. Insert the key just so—apply just enough twisting force to feel resistance—withdraw it gradually—wait for the resistance to disappear—then turn it all the way. This was my third try.

Maybe that's why I didn't see her coming. Just as the key finally turned, she came rolling around the corner like a tiny armored troop carrier. What happened when we collided was a perfect demonstration of the law of conservation of momentum. Body A came to a dead stop; Body B rebounded. Fortunately, Body B landed on his softest part. Body A stood horrified, mouth open, backpack clutched to her chest.

I looked up at her five feet, two inches. Julie. I might have known. "Never mind what they say on the artillery range," I grunted. "What you lack in mass, you make up in velocity."

"Professor Theophilus! I'm so sorry! Are you all right? Did you get hurt? Why aren't you getting up?"

Though I would have preferred to sit still, I got to my feet and limped into my office just to keep her from fretting. Gingerly, I sat down at my desk. She stood in the doorway uncertainly. "Are you sure you're all right? Can I do anything for you?"

"Yes, I'm sure, and yes, you can do something. First, you can pour me a cup of that cold coffee over there." She grimaced, but did as I asked. "Much better," I said, sipping. "Second, you can tell me what gives with the Girl-Shot-from-Cannon act."

"Girl shot from—oh," Julie's ears flushed pink. "I should have looked where I was going. But I'd just got my first essay back from Professor Thanatos, and when I saw my grade—I was so upset—I could hardly—" A new thought painted itself across her face. She sat down. "Professor Theophilus, since I'm here, would you do me a big, big favor?"

"I'm not sure I like the sound of that 'big, big.'"

"I know *you* didn't assign my essay. But would you read it anyway and tell me if *you* think it's really awful?"

"Julie, I try not to second-guess my colleagues' grading decisions."

"I'm not asking you to second-guess anything. But just *look* at this." She fished the essay out of her backpack and began to turn over the pages. "Page one, no comment. Page two, no comment. Pages three, four, five, no comment. See? Finally, bottom of page six, 'Weak argumentation, flaccid organization.' That's all. When I asked Professor Thanatos to explain, he just said, 'This is the university, Miss Terwilliger. You must sink or swim.'"

Yes, that sounded like Thanatos. I sighed. "Hand it over."

Five minutes passed as I penciled little check marks in the margins. "All right," I said finally, "let's talk." Julie perched herself nervously right on the edge of her chair.

"I won't tell you what grade I would have given the essay, but I can offer some basic critique."

"That's all I wanted."

"For starters, look at your introductory paragraph. There's no thesis statement."

"No what?"

"Thesis. You need to say what it is that you're going to prove. Even if you're not proving anything, you need to explain what question you're going to answer or what problem you're going to solve. But you don't do any of those things."

Her ears flushed again. "But I feel like I did. See, right here I say, 'My essay is about the existence of God.'"

"An 'about' statement is not the same as a thesis statement, Julie. It doesn't tell me what you want to accomplish in the essay. I could read the whole thing and still not know whether you'd succeeded."

"But I feel like the essay itself shows what I'm trying to accomplish."

"You may 'feel like' it does, but it doesn't. See here, in paragraph three you seem to be asking whether God exists. But in paragraph five you seem to be asking whether most people *think* He exists, and in paragraph eight you seem to be asking whether people who talk about God all mean the same thing. Is there some big question that links these three little ones together, or are you just meandering? You never tell me."

Her flush deepened and began to spread.

"Here's another thing," I said. "Look at the argument here in paragraph four. You seem to be reasoning 'all A are X, and all B are X, so all A are B,' but that doesn't follow. It's like saying, 'All dogs are four-legged animals, and all cats are four-legged animals, so all dogs are cats.' They aren't. Sometimes that's called 'faking the connection.'"

Her voice went up a full octave. "I haven't faked anything!"

"I don't mean you've tried to deceive. That's just one of the names for the fallacy."

"But I don't *feel* like I've committed a fallacy! You're just not being *fair*," Julie complained. Surprised, I looked up. The flush had reached her nose, and her eyes looked moist. "I feel you're just *looking* for things wrong."

I set down the pencil, pushed back my chair, hooked my thumbs in my pockets, and smiled. "Well, of course I am. You asked me to."

"After all the *effort* I put into the essay, you say it's no good!"

"I haven't yet said whether I think it's good or bad."

"I feel that's *exactly* what you're doing."

"But you asked me to do that too." I opened the drawer and pantomimed lifting out a tape recorder and setting it on the desk between us. "Rewind. Stop. Play. 'Professor Theophilus, would you read my essay and tell me if it's really awful?'"

"I'm sorry, I'm sorry!" she said. "I'm doing it again." I handed her a box of tissues. She blew her nose. "Just like I always do."

"What is it that you always do?"

"I *always* get like this when I'm criticized. Even when it's good for me and I've asked for it," she sniffled, "like today." She took another tissue. "Now that I'm in college, I'm *always* being judged. I love my subject, but sometimes I dread going to class. When I get criticisms from teachers or classmates, I just cringe." She wiped the corners of her eyes. "How can I stop being so hypersensitive?"

"Do you really want to know?" I asked. "It may feel like another criticism."

She blew her nose one more time. "Yes. Tell me."

"Then the first thing to consider is what you *gain* from being hypersensitive."

"What do you mean?"

"I mean that anyone who criticizes you is punished with emotional recriminations. You use them to shut people up before they've said all they meant to say, and to put the blame on them. That makes you feel better, but you pay a high price because you don't hear things you need to hear. Do you need the tissue box again?"

Her eyes went from my face, to the box, then back again. She shook her head. I smiled and continued.

"The second thing you need to do is to retrain your attention. When I criticized your work today, you didn't talk about the work, but about yourself."

"But everything I said was about the work!"

"Play back the tape again. Listen to what you said. You 'felt like' you had made your thesis clear. You 'felt like' you had reasoned well. You 'felt like' you hadn't committed fallacies. None of those feelings were in the essay. They were in you. Julie, no matter what you're feeling when someone criticizes your work, don't make your feelings the subject. Make the work the subject."

"You want me to think less about myself," she said. "But it seems to me that I don't think *enough* of myself. If I had more self-esteem, then I wouldn't be so hypersensitive."

I laughed. "Nothing you've said suggests that you lack confidence. What you lack is the humility to hear criticism. Your problem isn't humility, but the cardinal sin of pride."

"Pride? But—but *I* don't think I'm better than everyone else!"

"Irrelevant. Pride says, 'It's all about me.' That attitude can manifest itself in more than one way. If I'm selfish, I treat my *wants* as what it's all about. If I'm conceited, I treat my *worth* as what it's all about. You're not selfish or conceited, so you think you're not proud. Yet just a few minutes ago, you were treating your *hurt feelings* as what it's all about."

"You think *that's* pride?"

I shrugged. "It fits the definition. What do you think?"

Julie glanced at her watch, grabbed her backpack, and stood up. "I have to get to class, but I'll come back tomorrow. Will you hold on to my essay for me?"

"Certainly. Why?"

She paused on her way out and looked back through the door. "My arguments," she said. "I think I should hear the rest of your criticisms."

CHAPTER THREE

HOW DOES A CHRISTIAN REASON?

FAITH DOESN'T MEAN YOU DON'T REASON. IT MEANS REASONING A CERTAIN WAY.

As usual, Mary was rooting around in her backpack for something. She pulled out a coffee mug and set it on my desk.

"Another one?" I laughed.

She grinned too. "I know I'm always making off with your coffee mugs, but this one's different. It's the first I ever took. For three years I've been bringing it back and forth to your office. Now that I'm graduating, I thought I'd better return it for good."

So this was her farewell visit. I made myself busy with coffee to hide an unexpected rush of emotion. Mary had first visited my office three years ago to spout off about a classmate who had offended her by mentioning "the will of God." For some time now she had been a Christian herself, though I wasn't quite clear when or by what miracle of grace that had happened. I realized that I had come to think of her as something like a spiritual grandchild.

She sat pensively. I took my seat again.

"Professor—"

I waited.

"Professor T, faith is still pretty new to me. The other day I read what Paul says about being 'transformed by the renewing of your mind.' That made me think of something you said that first time I visited you. Do you remember? I'd said something stupid about 'blind faith.' You sort of winced and said, 'Not *blind* faith. Faith doesn't mean you don't reason, it means you ground your reasoning on the trustworthiness of God.' Or something like that."

"I remember."

"Well, I'm almost through with college, and I'm going to have to reason about a lot of things. Can you explain what you meant back then? How *does* a Christian reason? You started to explain one other time — but that was a long time ago and I didn't understand you very well."

"I'd be glad to try again. But you know some Christians might explain this a bit differently than I do."

"That's okay. Where do you start?"

"I start with the fact that God is the source of all truth, all knowledge. If you say that we can learn things by reasoning about them, I agree. But consider: Reasoning can't prove that reasoning works. Our confidence in reasoning is based on God. First He fashioned a world that makes sense, then He fashioned our minds so that it makes sense *to us*. The only reason we can trust reasoning is that the Fashioner Himself is reasonable. Do you follow me so far?"

"I think so. If that's true, then in a way, all real knowledge is — well, something like revelation. Right?"

"It's not *something like* revelation. It is revelation."

"I thought revelation meant the Bible."

"Revelation means whatever God makes known. The Bible is 'special' revelation — it's revealed to the people of faith. But He also reveals some things to *all* human beings, even apart from the Bible. That's called 'general' revelation."

"He reveals some things to nonbelievers? Like what?"

"Like the world's existence. You don't have to read the Bible to know that the world is real, though you might get confused about it. Like our own existence. Like the law of non-contradiction. Like 'one plus one is two.' Like 'equals added to equals are equal.' Like the fact that good is to be sought, and evil is to be avoided. Lots of things — the universal common sense of the human race. If God hadn't made these things known already, it's hard to see how the Bible could help us."

"But if we have this 'general' revelation already, then why *did* He give us the Bible? Was it to learn that *He* exists?"

"No, because even general revelation tells us that. Do you remember what Paul and Barnabas said in the fourteenth chapter of Acts?"

"When they were in Lystra? I was just reading that."

"Yes. They had just healed a man, and the pagan crowds thought they were gods. What did they say?"

"That the crowds should worship the true God instead."

"Right, but how were those pagans supposed to *know* about the true God?"

"I remember. They said that even in past generations, when God had allowed all the nations to walk in their own ways, He had left 'witness' to Himself among them. I didn't understand that. There weren't missionaries before Gospel times, were there?"

"There might have been, but that's not what they meant. Their words were 'Yet he did not leave himself without witness, *for he did good and gave you from heaven rains and fruitful seasons, satisfying your hearts with food and gladness.*'"

"I don't see how rain and fruit and gladness could witness to God."

"Don't you? Think. Why should there even *be* rain and fruit and gladness in the world? Why should there be a world at all? Creation witnesses to its Creator."

"Oh, I get it. 'The heavens declare the glory of God.'"

"Right. God left Himself other witnesses, too."

"Like what?"

"You might call one of them 'Godward longing.' Ecclesiastes says God has 'set eternity in the hearts of men.' We have an empty space in us that can only be filled by God."

"But how is that *knowledge?* There's a difference between longing for something and being told something."

"True. It's knowledge because it *does* tell us something—that none of our idols can save."

"You mean like that time when Paul was in Athens, and he saw an altar inscribed 'TO AN UNKNOWN GOD'?"

"Right. When he talked with them, Paul made a point of having seen it."

"But I thought we should use the *Bible* to reason with nonbelievers."

"Of course we want to teach them about the Bible. But it's not even biblical to *start* with the Bible. We should start where Paul did: with something they know already."

"Okay, I'm beginning to see it. We base our reasoning on the trustworthiness and—um—reasonableness of God. First He gives us general revelation, which is common ground even with nonbelievers. Then He gives us special revelation. That's where the Bible comes in. But you still haven't answered my question. What does the special revelation *add?*"

"Lots. The Athenians knew that there was 'An Unknown God,' but they still didn't know who He was."

"I get it. And I guess we also need the Bible to know about moral law, right?"

"I wouldn't say that. The Bible tells us *more* about moral law, but some knowledge of right and wrong is available even without it. He left witness among the nations not only to His reality, but to His moral requirements."

"That's kind of hard to believe."

"It shouldn't be. The Bible mentions at least three moral witnesses. First is the witness of conscience—what Paul calls the law 'written on the heart.' Second is the witness of the harvest—God has so arranged the world that eventually our deeds catch up with us. Third is the witness of our design. For example, you don't have to read the Bible to recognize that men and women are complementary to each other—each provides something lacking in the makeup of the other. Men can't do that for men, and women can't do that for women. Mary, *all* of these things are available for reasoning."

"But don't people deny all those things, Professor T?"

"Yes, but people aren't nearly as ignorant as they make themselves out to be. Were you, back in those days?"

"No. I knew all sorts of things that I didn't want to admit that I knew."

"So did I, when I was running from Him. But do you see what that means? If people hold down their conscience, perhaps with God's grace we can dredge it up. If they ignore the connection between deeds and consequences, we can connect the dots. If they avert their eyes from the obvious facts of design, we can call attention to them. By doing these things, we can reason about right and wrong even with people who don't yet share our faith."

"Okay, so we know *some* things already about God and His moral requirements. Then what does special revelation add?"

"It tells us *more* about God and His moral requirements. It makes even what we know already harder to ignore. Most important, it tells us the plan of salvation."

"I guess the reality of God might not seem like such good news if we don't know how to be reconciled with Him."

"Exactly. And His moral requirements might not seem like such good news if we know that we haven't lived up to them. We need the *real* Good News, the Gospel. We need to know that we can be for-given and made whole."

"I've surely learned what that's about," Mary said. She sat qui-etly for a moment, then said, "Professor T, even though I'm about to graduate, I feel that I'm only just now ready to begin."

"Of course you do, because you really are just beginning. You're a newborn child of Christ." I cleared my throat. "Oh, before you go—"

Opening the drawer, I pulled out an object tied with a bow and put it in her hands. "I just thought that since you're graduating, it's time you had one of these to call your own."

She smiled. "Thank you for the coffee mug, Professor Theophilus."

THE ANGRY TRIBE OF OPINIONATED PROFESSORS, PART 1

WHAT'S WRONG WITH BLATANT, UNREASONABLE BIAS, ANYWAY?

I usually skip lunch, but I needed the break, so I decided to try out the new food court in the atrium of Mammon Hall, the glass and marble business school building. There wasn't much variety—a Starblunks, another Starblunks, and a MacBurger's—but I gave in, grabbed a burger and coffee, and looked around the room. Just as I despaired of finding a place to sit, I heard someone calling, "Prof! Professor Theophilus!" Glancing in the direction of the voice, I saw Don, standing and waving with both arms. He was with Theresa and Peter, who were busy clearing a place at their table. It took me a few minutes to make my way to them through the crowd.

"Thanks," I told them. "There are so many people here, I thought I'd have to eat standing up."

"Don't thank us yet," said Peter. "We're going to make you work for that chair."

"Fair enough—considering how I make you work for your grades. What will you make me do, bus tables?"

"Worse," said Theresa. "We're going to cross-examine you."

"Am I in court, counselor?"

"That depends on what we think of your answers, witness. And we're not lawyers. We're judges."

"Sounds ominous."

"It should," said Don. "We're pretty steamed."

"At whom?"

"At the whole angry tribe of opinionated professors."

"Should I put on my war paint and feathers now?"

"Not you. You're okay. I'm talking about some of your opinionated colleagues."

"You mean some of them are even more opinionated than I am?"

"It isn't *whether* they're opinionated but *how* they're opinionated," said Peter.

"How are they opinionated?"

Peter looked surprised. "Don't you know?"

"I know how they strike *me*, but I'm not a student. How do they strike *you*?"

"They strike me as hateful," Don replied.

"Odious." Theresa this time.

"Morally obtuse." That was Peter again. "Like that guy in the news a few years ago who compared the 9/11 victims with Adolf Eichmann."

"Yes, I remember him. But I thought you were going to complain about our own faculty."

"We are," said Theresa. "Do you know Muito Egregious, the Spanish and Portuguese teacher?"

"Only by reputation."

"Well, I'm a Spanish major, and I can't avoid taking his courses."

"Does he live up to his name?"

"Sure does. He never misses an opportunity to be insulting or obscene — if possible, both at once. What he said this morning about Mother Teresa was unspeakable. I wish I could clean out my memory with soap."

"You think *you've* got it bad," said Don. "My Modern European teacher, Peccata Mundi, is a woman with a mission. Did you know that Christianity is responsible for all of the evils of the world? No? Well, that's what *she* says. Oppression of women? We did it. Slavery? Our fault. The Holocaust? We did that too, according to her. Stalin's purges? Before becoming a Communist, Stalin was a seminary student, so again we're to blame. Terrorism? We're just getting what we deserve."

"I can top that," said Peter. "My public policy professor, Prentice Schlange, isn't just nuts—he's a sadist. Yesterday he opened class by saying, 'All of you here are too intelligent to be pro-life, right?' A girl in front of me said, 'I'm pro-life.' He tore her down for five minutes."

"You didn't tell us about that," said Theresa. "What did he say?"

"He figured her reasons were religious, so the first thing he did was label her a 'fundamentalist.' It was downhill from there on. A lot of his diatribe was recycled quotations from other people. I recognized a couple of them, like H. L. Mencken's famous line about uneducable people who belong to the species *homo boobiens*. By the time my teacher was finished, the girl was in tears. Then he asked, 'Would anyone else like to say anything?' Of course no one else did, so he smiled nastily and said to her, 'It seems that you're a minority of one.'"

I raised a judicial eyebrow. "Are you saying that all of your teachers are like these three?"

"Yes and no," replied Theresa. "Not many faculty are that extreme. On the other hand, there's a persistent left-wing, antireligious bias in almost all of our classes. Sometimes mild, sometimes not."

"Make that anti-*Christian* bias," said Peter. "They hardly ever criticize, say, Hinduism or New Age religiosity."

Don said, "Unless you already know the material being taught, though, it's hard to pin it down. A lot of our classmates don't even notice a bias. They don't have anything to compare it with."

"I wouldn't say that," said Peter. "Most of them notice, but they just don't care. Know what I mean? 'Give me my degree and I'm out of here.'"

"But a lot of them *do* care," said Theresa. "They just don't know what they can do about it."

A silence fell. They seemed to expect me to say something. I asked, "Is this where my cross-examination begins?"

Theresa said, "That was just joking. But as a professor, you must have noticed the bias too."

"Of course. You should sit in on a faculty meeting sometime."

They laughed. "I guess your views aren't exactly common here," said Don.

"They're not as uncommon as they used to be."

"You mean there's a backlash?" he asked.

"I wouldn't put it so strongly. But there are cracks in the monolith."

"So how do *you* deal with opinionated professors?"

"That's not the right question, Don. I don't confront them as a student but as a colleague, as a fellow member of the faculty. The face that the problem presents to me isn't quite the same as the face that it presents to you, and the means available to you for dealing with it aren't quite the same as the means available to me."

"Okay, how can *we* deal with bias?",

"How large an answer do you want?"

He answered, "How large an answer do you have time for?"

I glanced at my watch and smiled ruefully. "Not very large."

"Okay, let's make the question smaller," said Theresa. "Just tell us how we can deal with teachers like Egregious, Mundi, and Schlange."

"All right," I replied. "To start with, tell me what it is about their behavior that you find so objectionable."

They looked at each other like I was crazy. "Isn't that obvious?" asked Peter.

"Pretend I'm stupid. The problem is—what? What kind of statements on their part are you objecting to?"

"Statements like the ones we told you about."

"Statements 'like' those. *What* are they 'like'? Characterize them."

"Haven't we done that? They're opinionated. Like we said."

"That won't do, Peter. As you also said, the problem isn't *whether* they're opinionated but *how* they're opinionated."

"But our teachers shouldn't be laying their points of view on us."

"If having a point of view is what you're objecting to, then your objection is hopeless. Every teacher has a point of view. It's impossible to teach and *not* have a point of view."

Don said, "Shouldn't our teachers be teaching us the *facts*?"

I answered, "The *goal* is to arrive at the factual, certainly. But there is no getting around the fact that at least at the beginning, there are different opinions about what the facts *are*. So don't complain to me that Professors Egregious, Mundi, and Schlange have opinions. Tell me what's wrong with the way that they *deal* with opinions."

"They're hateful," said Don.

I smiled. "You know, I've been accused of being hateful too."

"You? But you're — well, you're a Christian. You're *against* hatred."

"I am."

"Who accused you?" asked Theresa.

"A student who wandered in during Q and A, following a talk I gave several years ago at the Student Union. The talk was about constitutional liberties, and someone asked a question about laws that forbid discrimination on the basis of 'sexual orientation.' I remarked that 'sexual orientation' can mean many things, and I wondered where this trend would end."

"I was there," said Peter. "So?"

"The student came to my office afterward. Very bitter fellow. He accused me of a bizarre statement I hadn't made, told me I was bigoted and hateful, and said he was going to file a formal complaint with the people who run the Student Union speakers series."

"Did he?"

"I've never checked."

"Were you ever invited to speak at the Union again?"

"Of course not. Do you get my point?"

"I think so. Real hatred is wrong, but false accusations of hatred are too easy to use to censor opinions that people just don't want to hear."

"Right. That's the adversary's game. If I were you, I'd avoid getting caught up in it."

"So where does that leave us?" asked Theresa.

CHAPTER FIVE

THE ANGRY TRIBE OF OPINIONATED PROFESSORS, PART 2

THERE'S A RIGHT WAY TO TALK BACK, BUT USE YOUR HEAD.

Theresa had just asked, "So where does that leave us?"

I shrugged. "You tell me," I said. "Exactly what is *wrong* with the way that Professors Egregious, Mundi, and Schlange deal with opinions different than their own? I'm not asking the problem with their motives. I'm asking the problem with how they behave, with how they talk."

"The problem with their talk is that it's offensive," said Peter.

"That can't be right," said Theresa. "It's too much like saying that they're hateful."

"I don't see how," said Peter. "Hatred is about motive. It's all too easy to say that someone's motives are hateful just because you don't agree with what he says. We agreed that we don't want to play that game. But whether something offends isn't about motive. It's about how what he says comes across."

"But isn't it just as easy to say you're *offended* just because you don't agree with what he says as it is to say he's *hateful* just because you don't agree with what he says?" countered Theresa. "How is *that* game any better?"

Don said, "Reesi's right. Whether their talk offends anyone is beside the point. I think the problem is that it's biased against Christianity."

I asked, "So would you say that criticism of Christianity should be forbidden?"

"No-o-o," he quavered, "I wouldn't say *that.*"

I grinned. "I wouldn't either. But why not?"

He answered, "If we said that, then what would happen if the tables were turned and people of a different creed came to power?"

"Right," said Peter. "Maybe then nobody would be allowed to criticize Islam, or Voodoo, or whatever."

"The tables have *already* turned," said Theresa. "Isn't that why we're having this conversation? People of a different creed *are* in power in places like Post Everything University."

"What do you mean?" asked Peter.

"In our classes, nobody is allowed to criticize the secular humanist creed."

"Wait a moment," I said. "Go back two steps. Don, you said you wouldn't shut up people who disagree with you because in that case, if they ever got the power they might shut you up instead. Is that the only reason? If you had the power and you were *sure* of keeping it, *then* would it be okay to shut them up?"

He glanced at the others. "No," he said, "but I'm not sure why."

"Think it over."

After a few moments, he said, "There *is* a deeper reason. I'm trying to remember—it was in an author you assigned—a long time ago, in the first course I took with you. An early Christian writer. Lactose or something."

"Probably Lactantius. What about him?"

"*He* said there's a deeper reason. Because true faith can't be coerced."

Trying to suppress a smile, I handed him the book I had been carrying that morning and asked, "Is this the book you're trying to remember?" It so happens that I teach that course often.

Astonished, he looked at the spine. "That's it, all right. Magic! What chapter was it where he talked about that?"

"Try Book Five, Chapter 20."[5]

The chapters are short, so in a few seconds he found what he was looking for. He looked over at Peter and Theresa. "Um, do you all want me to read it out loud?"

"Do it," Peter said.

"'Religion cannot be imposed by force. The matter must be carried on by words rather than by blows, that the will may be affected.'"

"Keep going," said Theresa.

"All right. 'Let them unsheath—'"

"Who's 'them'?" asked Peter.

"He means nonbelievers. 'Let them unsheath the weapon of their intellect; if their system is true, let it be asserted.' And listen to this. 'For we do not entice, as they say; but we teach, we prove, we show.' A few lines down he says, 'For nothing is so much a matter of free-will as religion; in which, if the mind of the worshipper is disinclined to it, religion is at once taken away, and ceases to exist.'" A little self-consciously, Don laid the book down.

"That's cool," Peter said. "When did you say that guy wrote?"

Don looked at me. "Fifth century?"

"Close. Fourth."

"Anyway," said Don, "I think he nails it. This guy lived under persecution, right, Prof? The pagans tried to shut the Christians up. He didn't say, 'If only *we* had the power instead.' He said, 'That's not the way power should be used. Faith can't be coerced.' And he told the pagans, 'Go ahead, show your stuff. Bring out your arguments, and I'll bring out mine. Let's see who's more convincing.'"

"*That's* the problem with our angry and opinionated professors, isn't it?" asked Theresa. "It isn't their hatefulness. Or their offensiveness. Or the fact that they're against Christianity. It's that they *don't* allow argument."

"That's what I'm saying," said Don.

"Peter?" I asked.

"I agree. I take back what I said about offensiveness. Don and Reesi's answer is better."

"All right, group," I said. "I'll accept your answer to question one. The problem with the way the angry tribe of opinionated professors deals with opposing opinions is that they don't allow argument. Are you ready for question two?"

"I guess so," said Don. He glanced around for confirmation. The others nodded.

"Here's the question. What are you going to do about it?"

Theresa stalled. "What do *you* think we should do?"

"Me?"

"Yeah, c'mon, Prof," said Peter. "We were going to cross-examine *you*, remember? But you're cross-examining *us*."

"Give us a break," said Don.

"Since you ask," I said, "I think you should do what Lactantius did."

"You're being cryptic," said Peter.

"Not at all," I said. "Don, a moment ago weren't you telling us what Lactantius did?"

"Right. He challenged his adversaries to show their stuff."

"Well, then?"

"You can't mean for us to do *that*."

"Why not?"

Theresa answered for him. "We don't have enough stuff to show. Our professors know so much more than we do. That's why they're professors."

"They do know more," I answered, "but think back to the beginning of the conversation. You were explaining to me how Professor Egregious lives up to his name. Would you mind repeating what you said?"

"I said he never misses an opportunity to be insulting or obscene."

"You gave an example from this morning's class. His foul remarks about Mother Teresa."

"Yes, but don't ask me to repeat them. I don't even like to think about them."

"Of course you don't. And I won't. But when he made those remarks, was it the superiority of his knowledge that put you at a disadvantage?"

"No. It was his filthiness."

"Then it wasn't the inferiority of *your* knowledge that kept you from responding."

"What was I supposed to say?" she flashed. "You can't *refute* filthiness."

"No, but you can challenge it. You can deprive it of its power to intimidate."

"How?"

"Is it so hard to say, 'Professor, filthiness is not an argument'?"

"He's got you there, Reesi," said Peter.

Turning to him, I asked mildly, "How about you?"

"Me?" he squeaked.

"Sure. Why couldn't you challenge *your* professor—Schlange, isn't it?"

He cleared his throat. "My case is, um, different."

"How is it different?"

"He doesn't use obscenity. He shuts people up with humiliation. I told you how he humiliated the pro-life girl in my class yesterday."

"Refresh my memory."

"He tore her down for five minutes, then asked, 'Would anyone else like to say anything?' Dead silence."

"Why didn't you?"

"Why didn't I what?"

"Say anything."

"You mean I should have subjected *myself* to that treatment?"

"No, I mean you should have *contested* that treatment. A good start might have been asking, 'Sir, how do sarcastic remarks about *homo boobiens* prove your case about abortion?"

"As though *that* would shut up a bully like him."

"You'd be surprised. Professorial bullies are a lot like other bullies. They aren't prepared to be contradicted."

"And if it *doesn't* shut him up?"

"By pointing out that an insult isn't an argument, you put him in a dilemma. Either he presents you with a real argument—that's what you want, isn't it?—or he loses face."

"What difference does it make? I can't win by *argument*, even if my arguments are stronger. He controls the microphone."

"Who said you have to win?"

They glanced at each other again. I repeated the question. "Who said you have to win?"

Peter said, "I don't think I understand."

"Is the question difficult?"

"Isn't winning the *point*?"

"Certainly you should muster the best arguments you can, don't ever stop thinking that, not for a moment. But no, in a case like this winning isn't the point. The point is bearing witness."

"Now I'm even more confused," he answered.

I said, "So what if your professor isn't convinced? So what if he gets the last word? So what if he changes the subject? All you have to do is plant a seed."

Peter said, "But if the soil is rocky—"

"What do we know about which soils are rocky and which ones aren't? Does God tell us what uses He plans to make of our obedience? Besides, he's not the only person present."

Unexpectedly, his face was creased by emotion. "If I'd spoken up yesterday—I was only speaking of myself. I wasn't even thinking of that girl."

"The one your professor tore down?"

He nodded. Out of the corner of my eye I noticed that some obscure passion had imprinted itself on Don's face too.

"Aren't *we* a pack of mice," said Theresa. "In other parts of the world Christians die for their faith, and here we are, scared witless, just because a few opinionated professors might sneer at us in front of our classmates."

Don said, "We ought to find it *easy* to bear our crosses. They're hardly crosses at all."

"I don't think that line of thought is helpful," I said. "If your crosses weren't real crosses, then you wouldn't be so afraid to carry them. Don't worry about how light or heavy they are compared with the crosses other people bear. I'm not saying that you should dramatize your burdens, but you shouldn't disparage them either."

"I guess you're right," he said. "These are the crosses we're given. All we have to do is bear them."

"That, and one more thing."

"What?"

I didn't have to give the answer; Peter did. "Maybe help all the others bear theirs."

CHAPTER SIX

LEARNING TO THINK

LETTERS

LET US DO EVIL THAT GOOD MAY RESULT

Dear Professor Theophilus:

I am currently taking a neuroanatomy course, and part of the material covers ethical issues in neurology. One issue raised by our lecturer was using fetal tissue for neural grafting into terminally ill patients. The tissue used is from aborted fetuses, and usually three or four fetuses are required to get enough cells for one transplant. What do you think about the issue? I know that abortion is morally repugnant, but is the use of aborted fetal tissue in such transplants ethical?

Reply: Good question. To see how to approach it, consider a parallel. Suppose a killer offered to provide a hospital a steady supply of body parts, cut from his victims, for people who needed transplants. Should the hospital take him up on his offer? Of course not, and the fact that it would be "for a good cause" would make no difference. The purchase would not only be wrong in itself, but would provide the murderer with a financial incentive to commit even more murders.

The use of tissue from aborted babies for medical research is equally wrong, and for exactly the same reasons. When people suggest to us, "Let us do evil, that good may result," we must always refuse, as Paul did in Romans 3:8.

Peace be with you,
Professor Theophilus

WANTED: RELIGION PROFESSOR — MUST BE IRRELIGIOUS

Dear Professor Theophilus:

I'd like to know why there are two different versions of the creation story in Genesis. We studied creation myths in one of my English classes, and my professor said that the two different versions prove that the Bible is myth.

Reply: Your professor is not a logical thinker. Believers have always recognized that there are two versions of the creation story. If the two versions were inconsistent — for example, if one version said that God made Man in His image but the other version denied it — then your professor might have a case, but that's clearly not what we find, for the two versions are complementary. Each contributes its own insights.

The first one, Genesis 1:1–2:3, focuses on creation in general. It makes clear that God is the Creator, that there is no other Creator, that He was pleased by His creation, and that He made Man (both male and female) in His image. The second one, Genesis 2:4–2:25, expands upon the idea of Man being made in God's image. It emphasizes the original harmony not only between God and humanity, but between male and female humanity. The sequel, Genesis 3:1–3:24, explains how the first human beings, through rebellion against their Creator, lost both kinds of harmony, bringing terrible consequences upon themselves and all their descendants. In the rest of the Bible, we discover what God has done to rescue us.

I can't help reflecting that whenever I give directions to my house, I give two versions — one focusing on the names of the roads, the other on distances and landmarks. Sometimes I even give a third — "Now if you get lost, do this." By your professor's reasoning, I guess that proves that my house is a myth too.

Peace be with you,
Professor Theophilus

IS HISTORY ALL IN OUR HEADS?

Dear Professor Theophilus:

Most of my fellow students accept without a shadow of a doubt the saying "history is nothing more than a lie agreed upon." They think that no accurate historical account has ever existed or ever could because history is "written by the winners." In their view, the only history that matters is each person's subjective experiences. Since The Da Vinci Code *came out, I've run across this idea more and more.*

This view stymies me any time I try to discuss the reliability of the Bible and the events of Jesus' life. How can I logically and reasonably defend the fact that some history can be known with confidence? How can I make the Bible seem relevant to those who see all historical documents as biased texts written by "the winners"?

Reply: Your problem with your classmates is ridiculously easy in one way, but terribly difficult in another. Let's take the easy way first. They say that no historical claim has ever been accurate, and that no historical claim can ever be made with reasonable confidence. But wait! To say something about what has or hasn't "ever been" *is* to make a historical claim. So their own claim is historical too! Now if it's true that no historical claim has ever been accurate, then their claim that no historical claim has ever been accurate is also inaccurate. But in that case some historical claims *may* be accurate, which means that their view is *wrong*. Their opinion is self-refuting.

Here's another way to explode it. Their reason for thinking that no historical account can ever be trusted is that "history is written by the winners," and winners can never be trusted. But if it's true that the majority of the students at your school accept this view, then for the time being, *they* are the winners at your school, right? So their own premises prove that they can't be trusted. Who's left to trust? Well, people like you, who say that reasonable confidence *can* be placed in historical claims that are backed up by good evidence.

Still another way to demonstrate the absurdity of their position is to show that they don't believe it themselves. If they did, they would never place confidence in any historical account whatsoever. But they do. How do we know that? Because, as you said, they do place confidence in their own subjective accounts of the things that have happened. According to them, no other histories "matter," but these histories do. This is a good time to ask them what that means. When they say that their subjective histories "matter," do they mean that these histories can be reasonably accepted as true? If they answer "No," then they're claiming that it's reasonable to act on premises that it isn't reasonable to believe. That doesn't make sense. But if they answer "Yes," then they are admitting that we can place reasonable confidence in some historical claims after all.

The final way to undercut their position is more constructive. A lot of history really is unreliable, and we may as well admit it. But *how did we find out* that it was unreliable? We found out by examining the historical evidence. But if that's what we did, then not all historical reasoning is worthless after all. One has to proceed with caution, of course, scrutinizing the evidence and keeping a lookout for distortions, but that's not the same as utter skepticism. The moral of the story isn't that history is impossible, but that history is *difficult*. That shouldn't surprise us because everything worthwhile is difficult. Patience is difficult, love is difficult, plumbing is difficult—they all require sweat.

The same goes for talking with your classmates. The arguments I've offered may seem pretty obvious, but as I said at the beginning, your problem is easy in one way, fiendishly hard in another. Since the view that reality can't be known refutes itself, no one can swallow it just by making a mistake; anyone sharp enough to understand it is sharp enough to see through it too. But this implies that anyone who does swallow it must want to very badly. Now ask yourself: What sort of motive could be strong enough to make someone *want* to shut out the claims of reality? I know of only two: suffering so extreme that it produces insanity, and sin so impenitent that it produces insane ideologies. You're not just dealing with an intellectual problem, you're dealing with a spiritual one. So reason, reason, reason with your friends—but pray, pray, pray for them as well.

One last thing. I'm glad that you want to evangelize, but I hope that isn't your *only* reason for defending the knowability of the past. All truth belongs to God; it's worth knowing for that reason alone.

Peace be with you,
Professor Theophilus

WHEELS WITHIN WHEELS

Dear Professor Theophilus:

I've been struggling with faith versus reason—and whether I ought to say versus! In How to Stay Christian in College, *you criticize the common idea that faith hinders the search for truth because it gets in the way of reasoning. According to you, reasoning itself depends on a kind of faith, because the only way to prove that reasoning isn't hogwash would be to reason about it, and any such argument would be circular. It would take on trust the reliability of the very thing it was trying to prove reliable. For this and other reasons you conclude that it makes no sense to ask whether to have faith. "The only real question is which kind of faith to have. The wrong kind will hinder the search for truth — but the right kind will help."*

My question is, how do you choose which kind of faith to have? If reason itself requires a kind of faith, then are we choosing our faith based on the faith that we have yet to choose? Is there more than one type of faith, possibly? What can I do with these seeming circularities?

Reply: The circles do stop spinning. One thing that stops them is "first principles," self-evident principles which we accept not because we can prove them but because they are "known in themselves." Would you like examples? A first principle of arithmetic is that equals added to equals are equal. A first principle of what to do is that good is to be done and evil avoided. A first principle of logic is that no proposition can be both true and false in the same sense at the same time. You can't prove such things, but you can't *meaningfully* deny them either because you have to make use of them even to argue that they aren't true. Confronted with this fact, there are two ways to respond. You can deny them anyway, but that way lies madness. Or you can believe them. That's an act of faith, in the special sense that it isn't based on proof. But in a sane view of reasoning, it is a *reasonable* act of faith — an act of faith that is necessary for reasoning itself. If knowledge is what it is sane to believe, then it is also knowledge.

Faith decisions are involved in everyday experience too — not only in our relationship with God, but even in human relationships. How does a young man decide about a young woman, "This is the one?" If he is wise, he will carefully consider everything he knows about her — her character, her conduct, her commitments — before committing his faith to her. If he does all that, then his faith in her is reasonable. Yet isn't there something in that faith that goes beyond what proofs can tell him? Of course there is. Reason says, "So far as I can tell, this woman is true," but it can't prove that she is. Really trusting her—staking his life and future on her trustworthiness—is more than proving a theorem. Nevertheless there comes a point at which a young man is justified in trusting her, and even in saying, "I know her."

If that analogy doesn't help, try this one. You're standing at the window of a burning house. The fireman calls out, "Jump! I'm holding the net, and I'll catch you!" But alas! Your eyes are stinging with smoke and dazzled by the glare of the flames. You cry out, "I can't see you! I'm afraid! I can't jump!" He calls back, "It doesn't matter whether you can see me! I can see *you*! Trust me, and jump anyway!" Would jumping be reasonable? Of course. But does knowing this make jumping easy? Does it spare you the necessity of trust? Of course not. Reason can point you in the right direction, but faith is still a leap—in this case, literally.

So it is with our faith in God. Nothing in Christian faith is contrary to reason; in fact, faith is eminently reasonable because the world makes more sense if the Christian faith is true than if it isn't. Rationally, Christianity beats atheism hands down. Yet we still don't know everything, do we? We can't *see* God any more than you can see that fireman with the smoke in your eyes. So there is something more *even to reasonable* faith than reason alone.

I've given examples of reasonable faith. Unfortunately, you're right: There is such a thing as unreasonable faith—and there is such a thing as unreasonable refusal of faith. Consider that young man in love. He might place his faith in a young woman of bad character, against his better judgment. People do that sort of thing all the time. Or consider that building burning down. You might *not* make the leap of faith into the fireman's net, even though it is the reasonable thing to do. Refusing faith, you burn with the house, and you perish.

Here's a bonus. Think about the young man in love again. This time, suppose the young man said, "I refuse faith. I refuse to say that I know anything at all unless I have proof. I won't give myself to my beloved unless I can actually see her heart." That attitude is crazy for a lot of reasons, but the craziest thing about it is this: *By refusing faith, he is cutting himself off from the very knowledge he demands.* True, there are some things that he has to know before his trust in the young woman can be reasonable. But it's also true that until he trusts her, there are some things about her that he can never know. Trust transforms the relationship, making possible certain forms of personal knowledge that would have been impossible without it.

In this sense, too, faith is reasonable — and this too is true of our relationship with God. That's why the great Christian writer Anselm wrote *Credo ut intelligam*, which doesn't mean "I come to know, in order that I may believe," but "I believe, in order that I may come to know."

One day we will see God face to face, and then there will be no need for faith. Then we will know, even as we are known. In the meantime, faith is an utter necessity.

Peace be with you,
Professor Theophilus

I DON'T LIKE IT HERE

Dear Professor Theophilus:

I'm a freshman in college at a university run by a certain Christian denomination, but I really don't like it. The longer I'm here, the more I feel like I'm getting theology shoved down my throat. I'm not really in college with any particular goals in mind: I'm kind of just here because I'm not sure what else to do. So does it make sense to leave? I think the college experience has benefited me, but I find myself becoming more and more resentful of the "Christian" part of it. I have to take many more ministry/theology classes as a part of my general requirements, and I'm really not interested. I really need advice: I don't want to make a decision I'm going to regret, especially considering the investment.

Reply: The question you need to ask yourself is *why* you resent "the Christian part of it." No, I'm not scolding you. Your reasons for resenting the theology requirements may be either good or bad, but you have to find out what they are. Here are some of the possibilities:

1. The real problem is although you recognize the value of college, you're just not ready for college right now, and the theology requirements are an easy target for your resentment about everything in general.
2. The real problem is that you prefer a shallow faith, and you resent the theology courses because they urge you to cast your net in deeper waters.
3. The real problem is that although you do want a deeper faith, you resent the theology courses for pushing you faster than you can go.
4. The real problem is that something is wrong with the theology taught in those courses. It doesn't answer your questions, or it answers them poorly, or it just doesn't have the aroma of Christ.
5. The real problem is that your theology courses are designed for people who are going into church-related professions, and that's not your calling.

Don't answer quickly. Take all the time that you need. Think; ponder; pray. You need to be sure of your answer.

If the answer is number 1, drop out of college for awhile. Get a job, work hard, be responsible, save money. If you live at home, pay room and board. After a few years, think about college again. You may feel differently than you do now.

If the answer is number 2, try to understand why you *don't* want to cast your net in deeper waters. That's like preferring less life to more. Perhaps there is a professor or counselor at the college you could talk to about this.

If the answer is number 3, I suggest that you change schools — not to one that *doesn't* push you spiritually (we all need that kind of push), but to one that pushes at a pace you can keep up with.

If the answer is number 4, you should probably consider not just a different school, but a different denomination. Notice that I said "consider"; I'm not telling you to do it. By all means hold on to Christ, but seek a place where you can find *all* of His truth.

If the answer is number 5, look for a university where the theology requirements are geared to people more like you — people who are serious about their faith, but not called to professions in the Church.

Probably, possibly, if! I hope you weren't looking for a *simple* answer, because I haven't given you one. But maybe I've guided you to the right questions.

Peace be with you,
Professor Theophilus

DOES IT EVER GET BETTER?

Dear Professor Theophilus:

I'm pursuing a Ph.D. in English literature at a secular research university. For the most part my professors and colleagues are very open to my academic discussions of faith. I've found a local community of believers and joined a weeknight discussion group organized by the church. I really enjoy interacting with both Christians and nonbelievers in an academic setting. I like my field in itself, I enjoy teaching, and I've had the joy of seeing many of my friends become Christians as they interacted with thoughtful believers trying to be faithful in the academy.

All the same, I think about quitting the field weekly, maybe daily. Everyone in my program who takes work seriously at all seems to be neglecting friends and family and sleeping just five to six hours a night, just to get by. The sheer amount of work the program expects of students is incredible.

I'd like to have more time to be involved in my church, do volunteer work, maybe even cook a meal and enjoy it with friends. Though I'm fighting, I can also feel the burden of work stifling my relationship with God. It's really hard to do more than skim through a psalm in the morning and then start work. I take Sundays off, but it's hard to sustain whatever thinking I do about God throughout the week.

I guess what I'm asking is, does it ever get better? Will I ever have more time? Or is the graduate school lifestyle the same one I can expect in my academic career?

Reply:[6] Of course it's possible that you shouldn't be in graduate school, but you don't give much reason for thinking that this is the case. To start with, yes, it gets better. Frankly, though, it doesn't sound too bad for you now. You obviously find time for worship and other church activities several times a week. You obviously have time for friends, or you couldn't have had the joy of seeing "many" of them turn to Christ. You just want *more* of these good things. I can hardly blame you, but we can't have everything at once. What about losing sleep? Five hours is a little stiff, but six hours a night, at your age, for a few years, doesn't sound so bad to me. People who are in at the start of something new and big often lose sleep. Newlyweds do. New parents do. People beginning new careers or businesses do. People organizing volunteer ministries do. People in love do. Converts do. Should we be surprised that grad students do too?

I said a few moments ago that it gets better. Let me fine-tune that statement. It *can* get better, but that depends largely on you. Here are two thoughts that might help you.

First, about grad school itself. Needless to say, it isn't easy, but even so, many grad students work harder and lose more sleep than they need to. Ironically, the commonest reason is that they're so smart. All through high school and college, they were the ones who breezed by while others had to toil. Grad school is often the first time in their lives that they've really had to work the way other students always had to. Suddenly they're forced to learn the time management habits that everyone else learned years earlier. Put all this together with the fact that for the first time in their lives, everyone around them is just as smart as they are, and what do you get? A recipe for insecurity, an urge to overwork, and a motive *not* to take the time to learn the habits that would make it all easier—those would take too much time to learn! You keep telling yourself that you don't have time to sleep because you have so much to do. But the less you sleep, the slower you work—and the more the work piles up, the less you sleep. Naturally, you get sick. The prospect of losing time to illness terrifies you, so you refuse to take time out to rest. Because you do refuse, the illness lasts for weeks instead of days, and you lose more time still. May I point out the obvious? None of this is necessary. It's driven by anxiety, not need.

Second, about spiritual discipline. The sanctification of everyday life is difficult; *everyone* finds it hard to sustain a focus on God through-out the week, not just grad students. Having too much work makes it hard—how right you are! But believe me, *not* having enough work makes it harder still. I commend you for wanting more quiet time to pray, but you already have far more than you think. You can pray while you're walking to school; you can pray while you're riding the bus; you can pray while you're making your dinner. True, you won't always be able to pray in *words*—you'd find it hard to do that while talking with your thesis supervisor—but you can have a prayerful spirit even then.

When Paul writes, "Pray constantly"—literally, "without ceasing"—I don't think he's talking about having a longer quiet time, though that's good too.[7] I think he's talking about the cultivation of an interior quietness of soul that makes it possible to pray literally all the time. May I once again point out the obvious? Progress in interior quietness will also help you in time management because the place that anxiety once filled is more and more filled up by God.

As I said before, perhaps you shouldn't be in graduate school—perhaps you aren't as well suited to the academic life as you seem to be—but I don't think so. I think your problems can be fixed. Yes, it gets better, even when it gets harder, as sometimes it will. That's how the path goes.

I don't mean the path of scholars, though scholars should follow it too. I mean the path of God.

Peace be with you,
Professor Theophilus

IS COMMON SENSE UNCHRISTIAN?

Dear Professor Theophilus:

In some of your writing about relationships, you offer common-sense arguments to bolster your case, yet you never cite a single passage of Scripture. I find this irresponsible.

Reply: Your notion that Christians have no business making arguments about matters not explicitly mentioned in Scripture is silly and worse than silly.

In the first place, it isn't Scriptural; Scripture exhorts us not only to be obedient to the Word of God, but to practice Wisdom. In the second place, it's pernicious. If it were really "irresponsible" to exhort Christians concerning something which the Bible doesn't mention, then I shouldn't condemn child molestation, self-mutilation, or playing "chicken" with other cars on the expressway, and I shouldn't affirm that the square root of sixteen is four. I'll say one thing for your opinion about common sense: It's a good way to keep from gaining any.

You should read the next letter too.

Peace be with you,
Professor Theophilus

GETTING WISE

Dear Professor Theophilus:

Proverbs talks a lot about the importance of getting Wisdom. I looked up "wisdom" in my dictionary and it just says "knowledge," but I know it must mean more than that. So what does the Bible mean by Wisdom?

Reply: Good question. Wisdom is the perfection of knowledge; it means seeing everything in the light of God. If knowledge were an arch, Wisdom would be the capstone, completing it and giving it strength. In calling Wisdom the perfection of knowledge I don't mean that it's just a collection of true beliefs. That's included, but it's more: a deeply engraved orientation of the whole intellect, the virtue that enables you to fulfill the commandment to love God with all your mind.[8] By the way, Wisdom is inseparable from right action. If it's just in your head, not also in your hands, feet, mouth, and eyes, it isn't Wisdom. And although it's a gift, it's not a cheap one. We could never achieve it without grace, but we have to hunger and thirst and labor for it too.

According to the book of Proverbs, "the fear of the LORD is the beginning of knowledge, [but] fools despise wisdom and instruction."[9] So what is the fear of the Lord? This is the trembling awe that comes from the presence of God, whose love is a consuming fire. You might say that Wisdom is *awful* knowledge, taking "awful" in its original meaning, "full of awe." To despise the fear of God is to despise knowledge itself. A mind not in awe of Him may know all sorts of details—like a man examining a painting with a microscope, micrometer by micrometer—but will never know the picture as a whole. The world may call that Wisdom, but it isn't what God has in mind.

Of course Wisdom is found in the written Word of God, but Scripture teaches that God has also spoken Wisdom into the design of His creation. This is something we tend to forget. It was by Wisdom, says Proverbs, that He founded the earth; by understanding that He established the heavens; by His knowledge that the deeps broke forth, and the clouds dropped down the dew.[10] We are commanded to pay attention, and in another passage the command becomes a warning, from the mouth of Wisdom herself: "And now, my sons, listen to me: happy are those who keep my ways. Hear instruction and be wise, and do not neglect it. . . . For he who finds me finds life and obtains favor from the Lord; but he who misses me injures himself; all who hate me love death."[11]

The New Testament identifies Wisdom with the Eternal Logos, who became incarnate in Jesus Christ and who makes His home in us through the Holy Spirit. "Logos" means both "reason" and "word"—the power and activity of Wisdom, and the way in which Wisdom is communicated to us. That's why the opening verses of the Gospel of John are translated, "In the beginning was the Word, and the Word was with God, and the Word was God." John goes on to say, "He was in the beginning with God; all things were made through him, and without him was not anything made that was made. In him was life, and the life was the light of men."[12] These words don't cancel out the Old Testament teaching about Wisdom; they complete it. To ignore the unspeakable gift of such Light from the Father of Lights is to turn down life itself and put ourselves in gravest peril.

This is lofty stuff, but it's also an everyday reality. Wisdom purifies and sanctifies even our common sense. Would you like a few humdrum examples? Read some of the letters about college relationships, at the end of the next section.

Peace be with you,
Professor Theophilus

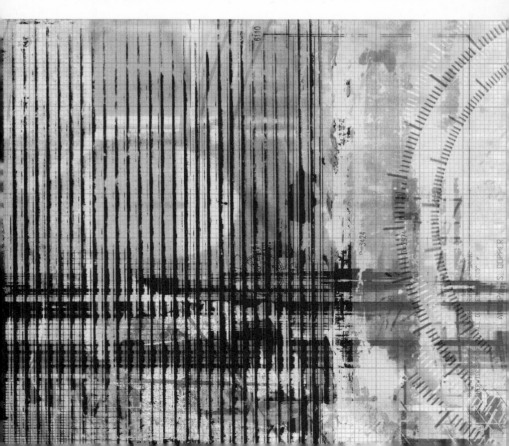

COLLEGE
RELATIONSHIPS STUFF

WHAT THIS SECTION IS ABOUT

Ask Me Anything 1 began with a section called "Girl and Guy Stuff," and I deal with plenty of girl and guy stuff here too. But the topic of college relationships is bigger than relationships between men and women. It includes a lot more.

Like friendships. Like roommates. Like wise trust, crazy trust, and loss of trust. Like forgiveness and its difference from forgetfulness. Like compassion and its difference from its counterfeit.

Whenever we talk about relationships we're dealing with what kind of people we are, what kind of people we're turning into—and what kind of people we ought to be turning into, which isn't always the same thing.

WHY AM I STILL BEING PUNISHED?

TWO BAD THINGS HAPPEN WHEN YOU HURT SOMEONE. FORGIVENESS ERASES ONE OF THEM, BUT WHAT ABOUT THE OTHER?

"Professor Theophilus?"

"Yes? Oh, hello!"

"I'm Brooke. I'm sure you don't remember me—"

"I do remember you. You were with Jordan at the annual university picnic." Jordan had been around a *lot* of girls at the annual picnic, but that's another story.

She sighed dramatically. "I'm so relieved. I knew you knew Jordan."

"Is something wrong with Jordan?"

"Not with him, with us. But *because* of something—actually, no, because of something *I*—anyway, I was hoping you might be willing to talk to me, because you know him. Jordan trusts you, and I need to talk with someone *old.*"

She covered her mouth with her hand. "I mean more experienced in life."

I smiled.

She added, "And you're a Christian and everything."

"And everything. What's the problem?"

"Now that I'm here, I'm a little embarrassed to tell you—it's about—"

"Your relationship with Jordan."

"How did you know?"

"I thought that was what you just told me."

"Oh. Yes. Well, I think I've made a big mistake with him. In our relationship. Such as it is."

"Back up. What exactly *is* your relationship? At the picnic, he introduced you as a special friend, but—"

"I know, he calls everyone a special friend."

I chuckled. She smiled nervously.

"I guess you'd say we're girlfriend and boyfriend," she said. "Since the picnic we've been seeing each other. Or we were."

"You've broken off?"

"I'm not sure," she hedged. She had exactly the look that my cat gets when she's trying to work up the nerve to jump through the door and come in.

"It's like this. Jordan—this is so embarrassing. Well. Jordan has a problem. It's, like, a flaw. A spiritual problem. What you'd call a beseeking—bespeaking—besettling sin."

"A besetting sin."[13]

"One of those. But I'd better not say more. Because that's the problem." She took a breath. "See, I happened to tell a few friends about it."

I raised my eyebrows. "You *happened* to tell them?"

"I mean, I told them."

"You told them it was Jordan?"

"I said 'my boyfriend,' but they all knew who I meant."

"Let me guess. Two weeks later, Jordan called you up and asked, 'Why have you been broadcasting my personal problems to everyone in the world?'"

"Only a week later. How did you know?"

"Wind blows, water flows, gossip gets around."

"I only told a few people."

"A few?"

"Only Amber, Ashley, Kala, Becca, Melissa, Danielle, and MacKenzie."

"That's a big few."

"But they said they wouldn't tell!"

"Telling is what people usually do with gossip."

"It didn't *seem* like gossip. They're my *friends*. Don't friends *tell* each other things?"

"Does that make it not gossip when they do?"

"Besides, they're not just *any* friends. They're my accountability group."

"How did Jordan discover that you'd told them?"

"The guys in *his* accountability group started ragging on him. Amber told Julie, who told Zack, who—you probably get the picture."

I nodded.

"I thought, isn't that what an accountability group is *for*? You know, 'Confess your sins one to another.' Isn't that what it says in the Bible?"

"What sins of yours were you confessing?"

She stared at me. "What?"

"You quoted the Bible, 'Confess your sins one to another.' What sins of yours you were confessing?"

"I wasn't confessing my sins."

"Whose were you confessing?"

"I guess I was confessing Jordan's." She looked morose. "Okay. I know I messed up with him. Actually I'd figured that out already, from how he acted."

"Was he upset?"

"*Really* upset. For weeks and weeks."

"Did you apologize to him?"

"Not right at first, but I did later."

"Has he forgiven you?"

She hesitated. "He says he has."

"Do you believe him?"

"Yes. Actually, yes, I do. He means it. I'm sure."

"That's good. Have you spoken to God about it?"

"Yes. I think He's forgiven me too."

Her face clouded and reddened. I waited for her to speak again.

She finally said, quaveringly, "Professor Theophilus, if I'm forgiven, *then why am I still being punished?*"

I sipped from my coffee cup to give myself time to think. "Who is punishing you?"

"Jordan. God. Both."

"Start with Jordan."

She sniffled and nodded.

"Is he treating you with resentment?"

"That's what's so awful. I could sort of understand if he did, because it would mean that he hadn't forgiven me." She pulled a tissue from her backpack and held it in readiness. "Actually he's been kind and understanding."

"But?"

"You'd think that if he really forgave me, the relationship would be just like it used to be. But it isn't. I feel it."

"How is it different?"

"There's a distance between us. It wasn't there before. He's not *trying* to put it there like some people do when they're angry. It's just there."

"Why do you think it's there?"

"Because he can't forget." She blew her nose. "I thought when you forgave, you were *supposed* to forget."

"No, I'm afraid that forgiving and forgetting aren't the same."

"Why not?"

"Sometimes forgetting isn't wise."

"When I was at my sister's house," Brooke said, "I broke down and cried, and she made me tell her what I was upset about. She said that if Jordan can't forget, then he must not really have forgiven me. But I *know* he forgave. So why *can't* he forget?"

"Think of it this way. Suppose one day a friend gives you a lift in his car, but he frightens you by cutting into traffic at high speed. Afterward he sincerely apologizes."

"Uh-huh." She nodded.

"You forgive your friend, but you know that his bad driving is habitual, and you're afraid he might do something crazy like that again. So the next time you need a lift, what makes more sense — to catch a ride with him, or to catch a ride with someone else?"

"To catch a ride with someone else."

"I agree. Now think. You haven't forgotten the way he drives. Does that mean you haven't forgiven him either?"

"I guess not, but that's different. In that story, if I don't remember I might get hurt. I don't see how *Jordan* could — oh."

"You do see?"

"Yes. He might be afraid that I'll blab his confidences again. He might be thinking that he can't trust me anymore. So there's a distance between us. Do you think that's it?"

"Let's say it's very probable. My point, though, isn't about what may be going through Jordan's mind. It's that forgiven sins have consequences too. That doesn't mean they're not forgiven."

"That doesn't change anything," said Brooke. "You can call it a 'consequence' if you want to, but it still feels like punishment." She stuffed the used tissue into her backpack, pulled out another, and buried her nose in it. "You probably think I'm being silly to talk that way."

"No, I think you're being accurate."

She looked up. "You do?"

"Yes. It *is* a kind of punishment."

"What do you mean?"

"A punishment is something you suffer as a result of sin. Isn't that what you're experiencing?"

"Yes. But I said it *felt* like punishment. How can it *be* punishment? Jordan isn't *trying* to punish me."

"Sin results in two kinds of suffering, Brooke. One kind has to do with guilt — it happens because what we've done is *wrong*. The other has to do with consequences — it happens because what we've done causes *harm*, to us or to others. Forgiveness erases the penalty of guilt, but something else is usually necessary to erase the penalty of consequences."

"I think I need an example."

"You burn down someone's house. He forgives you; your guilt is no longer written on his slate. That takes care of one penalty. But does it repair the damage?"

"No."

"So you suffer the further penalty of, say, building him a new home. Or giving him yours."

"I get that. One penalty is guilt, the other is damage. But how does that apply to me and Jordan?"

"Which penalty is confusing you?"

"I understand the penalty of guilt. He forgave me, and I think God forgave me. It's the other one I don't get, the penalty of damage. Are you talking about the damage to the relationship — the loss of trust?"

"Partly. There are two other kinds of damage too."

"I can think of one kind. Damage to Jordan. I hurt his feelings."

"You may have hurt more than his feelings. It's a lonely thing when someone we trust violates that trust. We usually find it a little harder to trust *anyone*, which is lonelier still. Do you think Jordan might be suffering those kinds of wounds?"

Her face betrayed shock. "Nothing like that even crossed my mind."

"And then there's the damage you did to yourself."

"*I'm* lonelier, that's for sure."

"I'm sure you are, but that's not what I mean. Vices and virtues are like stalagmites and stalactites. They're built up in our souls little by little, by the acts and choices we make every day. Every act of courage makes us inwardly more courageous; every act of cowardice makes us inwardly more cowardly. Every act of self-control makes us inwardly more self-controlled; every act of self-indulgence makes us inwardly more self-indulgent. Do you understand?"

"I thought virtues came from God's grace."

"Without God's grace, we're helpless. That's true. But the principle applies here too because we have to accept that grace. Every time we cooperate with it, we become inwardly more cooperative toward it, and every time we resist it, we become inwardly more resistant to it. Now do you see where I'm going?"

"I'm not sure."

"We were talking about how violating Jordan's trust damaged your soul. Reason the way I did about courage, self-control, and cooperation with the grace of God. But about trustworthiness."

"I think I get it. Every time we honor someone's trust, we become inwardly more worthy of trust. And every time we violate someone's trust—" Brooke's face changed color.

"Go on."

"We become a little less worthy of trust."

"*That's* how you damaged yourself."

"How can I repair all that damage?"

"You tell me."

"By showing that I can be trusted."

"Not just showing."

"By becoming more worthy of trust."

"How?"

"By—I guess—by honoring the trust people place in me. Little by little. Choice by choice. But Professor Theophilus—"

"Yes?"

"Won't that take a *long time?*"

"It might."

"And even if the damage is repaired in *me*, it seems to me there's no guarantee that it will be healed in *him* or in the *relationship.*"

"There's no guarantee. That sort of thing lies in the providence of God."

"But I've *prayed* to God about it. Professor Theophilus, I know He forgave me. He erased the penalty of guilt. Do you think He might erase the penalty of consequences too?"

"Do you mean in the long run or in the short?"

"Both!"

"In the long run, He promises to wipe every tear from the eyes of those who follow Him. But that's in heaven. In this life He promises only help."

"Why just *help*? Why won't He just *fix* things?"

"Presto, change-o! Just like that?"

"Yes! Just like that! Why *not*? Why *shouldn't* He?"

"Would it be good for us if He did?"

"How could it *not* be good?

"For one thing, sometimes we need to go on suffering one consequence of sin a little longer in order to recover from a different consequence of sin. One pain may be medicine for the other."

"That sounds *crazy.*"

"Is it? Right now you're suffering from the wound your act gave to your relationship with Jordan. But suppose you weren't. Suppose that wound had healed instantly. In that case, would you even be thinking about the wound that it did to your soul—about the bleeding hole it made in your worthiness to be trusted?"

That brought her up short. In a different voice, she said, "Maybe not."

For a few moments she was silent. Then she asked, "Is there *anything* I can do to make things better? I mean besides trying to be more trustworthy. And besides asking for grace. And, I guess, besides doing a better job of repenting than I think I did before."

"I think there is."

"What?"

"We're Christians, Brooke. Because of Christ's suffering for our sins, suffering ought to mean something different to us than it does to other people. It can unite us more closely to Him. So when you pray, offer your suffering to the Father. Offer it in communion with all Christians, to be united with the suffering of His Son."

"How could I unite my suffering with His?"

"He does it. Just let Him."

"Then does it go away?"

"No."

"I don't understand."

"You don't have to. He does."

She hesitated. "I could try."

"That's enough."

She gave me an odd look. "This isn't what I wanted from God."

"No—"

"But I think it might be better."

I smiled.

CHAPTER NINE

ROOMMATE WEIRDNESS

THEY GOT ALONG GREAT—UNTIL THEY WERE TESTED

As I was leaving the student Christian fellowship meeting, Don ran up from behind and matched his step to mine. "Hi, Professor Theophilus," he said, "Headed across campus?"

"All the way. You too?"

"Yeah, I thought I'd catch a bite at the Edge of Night." That was an eating hangout on the western edge of the Post Everything University campus; we were on the east. "Your talk was right on the nose."

"Thanks; I was afraid that the topic of 'Relationships' might be too big."

"No, it was fine. I just wish I'd heard that talk *last* year."

"Relationship problems of your own, eh?"

"You said it."

"Best friend? Girlfriend? Parents?"

"Roommate. Actually housemate."

"How bad?"

"Bad."

When I chuckled, Don objected. "Don't tell me *you* think it's funny, Professor T. It's bad enough that everyone else thinks so."

"It was a sympathetic chuckle," I said. "I was only amused by your answer. Not 'Very bad.' Not 'Extremely bad.' Just 'Bad.' That says it all."

He sighed. "I guess it does."

"How did the trouble begin?"

"That's the funny thing. See, we got along great before we moved in together."

"Naturally," I replied. "If you hadn't got along so well, you wouldn't have had the idea."

"I guess not. It never occurred to either one of us that there might be anything more to living together than sharing rent."

"You didn't work out ground rules, like the kind I discussed in my talk?"

"I never even thought of doing anything like that. But if I had, I would have told myself that it wasn't necessary."

"Why?"

"You know," he said. "We shared the same values and all that."

"Was your housemate a Christian?"

"Well, no."

"Then what made you think he shared your values?"

"He'd never been in trouble or anything. He didn't try to get me in trouble. He didn't get drunk or do drugs. He didn't sleep with his girlfriend. I never even saw him park in a No Parking zone."

I smiled. "There's more to sharing values, Don, than sharing the same list of 'don'ts.'"

"I know that *now*," he answered. "But I didn't then. It's like you said in your talk. If a person doesn't live *for* anything, then his good habits are just good habits. He doesn't have any reason not to change them for worse ones."

"And did he?"

"Did he what?"

"Change them for worse ones."

"Man, did he ever. First his friends started hanging around all the time and eating all our food. They didn't get along with my friends, so pretty soon my friends got fed up and stopped coming around."

"Did you say anything to your housemate?"

"No. I couldn't see myself telling him to get new friends just to please me—do you know what I mean?"

"I do. Then what happened?"

"Then they *all* began to change."

"How so?"

"First in their conversation. It was like—I don't know how to explain. I noticed the effect on me before I realized what was causing it. See, when I was with them, I found it harder and harder to be myself."

"Oh?"

"Yes. Christianity was never mentioned, but somehow the atmosphere changed from *not* being Christian to being *anti*-Christian. And then there was this suction."

"Suction?"

"Yes, I was getting *pulled*. I found myself saying things I didn't believe, just to be able to converse. It was weird."

"So what did you do?"

"I started spending less and less time at the house."

"Really?"

"Yeah, I did my studying at the library and came home just to wash and sleep."

"So control of the situation passed more and more to your housemate."

"I guess it did."

"Then what?"

"My housemate and his friends started leaving things everywhere. Like bottles. I never knew just a few guys could pack away so much beer."

"I thought you said he didn't drink."

"Well, he started. And another thing. He started resenting it when I went to my student Christian fellowship or to church. Sunday mornings he'd unplug my alarm clock. When I overslept and got angry, he'd think it was funny."

"That must be frustrating," I said.

"Not anymore. That's all stopped. Now he's got a better amusement."

"A better one?"

"Uh-huh. About a month ago his girlfriend started hanging around even more than his friends. Then another change began to happen. The more she came around, the less his friends did. But she was there all day—and pretty soon, all night, too."

"Yes, I thought that might be part of it. Both you and your housemate started out chaste, but as a Christian, you have reasons to stay that way that he hasn't—and you also have help that isn't available to him."

"But I still haven't told you the worst, Professor T."

"What's that?" I asked.

"She's starting to come on to *me*. At least I think she is. I don't know if it's a joke, or what."

"Doesn't your housemate object?"

"He doesn't know! See, she hangs around the house even more than he does now. It's like she doesn't have a life. Sometimes I come home late, and he's not there, but she is. And I'm tired, but I'm afraid—this is so ridiculous—I'm afraid to—"

"To go to bed?"

"Right! I'm afraid I might wake up *with her in it*."

"I can see why some of your friends might find the situation amusing."

"But it's not! I can't live like this!" he cried.

"No, you can't," I sympathized.

"Prof, how can I fix this situation?"

We walked the next fifty feet in silence.

"Did you hear me, Professor Theophilus?" Don finally asked.

"Yes, Don, I was thinking about your question," I told him. "But I don't think there is anything you can do."

"Not *anything*? But it isn't fair!"

"No, not at all."

"I pay my half of the rent, I pull my weight, I do my share—am I supposed to just accept the situation and live in it?"

I glanced at his face. "Haven't you already addressed whether you can live in it?"

"I said I couldn't."

"And you were right."

"But if I can't live in it, and I can't change it—"

"Then there's only one other alternative."

"To lose my share of the deposit money and move out?"

I laughed. "If you lose only money, Don, you'll have done well." He looked puzzled for a moment, then his face reddened slightly and he laughed too. I went on. "Do you have a friend you can stay with for the next few nights, while you look for a new place?"

"Uh—yes, probably—I could call around," he said. "But if I found a new house and a new housemate, wouldn't I just wind up in the same mess as with the old one?"

"Why should you assume that?" I said. "Not unless you make the same mistakes. What should you do differently this time?"

"I guess I need to find someone who doesn't just avoid the things I avoid, but who also lives for what I live for."

"Then what?"

"Isn't that enough?"

I chuckled again. "If my talk on 'relationships' is really so forgettable, it must have been poorer than you thought. Doesn't the expression 'ground rules' ring a bell?"

"Sure. But do I need ground rules even with another Christian?"

"Absolutely. We're fallen; Christians can drive each other crazy too. A Christian is under new management, true, and undergoing repairs. But while the repairs are going on, the air is full of dust and there are nails all over the floor. By all means find a housemate who shares your faith, but reach some understandings with him about all the practical aspects of living together too."

During our talk we had walked all the way from the east side of campus to the west and were approaching the Edge of Night. For the last two blocks Don was silent. At the door of the hangout, just as I was about to turn aside to pick up my car from the faculty parking lot and go home, he spoke again.

"Professor Theophilus, there's something else I wonder if I could talk about with you. Could I get you a cup of coffee or something?"

I glanced at my watch, then his face. He looked even more uneasy than he had when he was telling the tale of his troubles with his housemate. "Yes, I have time for a cup. Nobody's expecting me for a little while. What's it about?"

"I'll explain after we've found a place to sit down. It's just that when my housemate's girlfriend was coming on to me—I didn't give in, but—let's say it raised some questions in my mind."

I passed my hand over my face. "Oh, is *that* all?" I grinned. "I'm sure we can deal with *that* in five minutes."[14]

FALSE COMPASSION

ISN'T COMPASSION A CHRISTIAN THING? THEN HOW COULD IT EVER BE WRONG?

A Christian student group called CrossTalk had invited me to speak about "rules of engagement," which turned out to mean relationship ethics. Sometimes when you address a group, the questions are about what you talked about. But sometimes they have nothing to do with it.

I was finishing up.

". . . that both models of relationship leave something to be desired. You're a part but not *just* a part, an individual but not *just* an individual. Any questions?"

I already knew it was a flop. Maybe the reason a prophet is without honor in his own country is that he does a better job prophesying when he's not in it. I'm not a prophet, but it's like that with speakers too.

Nobody said a word. Kala, the program chairman, looked unhappy. Some students had their eyes closed.

"Um. Professor Theophilus?"

A question. Jump on it. "Yes, go ahead."

Tall guy, third row. "Could you explain what you said about 'false compassion'?"

Had I said *anything* about false compassion? If I had, I didn't remember.

"Hmmm, yes. Would you tell me which remark about false compassion you're asking about?"

In the back of the room, the faculty sponsor, Bob Loons—a friend of mine—was grinning and shaking his head. I knew I'd be ribbed afterward about this dismal performance.

"Well, I didn't understand any of them," said the tall guy. "Would you just explain what false compassion *is?*"

My friend made a noise that I thought was muffled laughter.

"That I can do," I replied. "The word 'compassion' can mean two different things. The *virtue* of compassion is sympathizing in the right way, for the right things, and doing the right thing about it. The *feeling* of compassion is sympathy *period,* and it's not always right. When it isn't, it's called 'false compassion.'"

Several students began to look faintly interested. The most wide-awake-looking girl in the room said, "Could you give an example?"

"Sure," I said. "Aunt Mary says to the parents of a greedy little boy, 'How could it be wrong to give my poor nephew a fifth piece of chocolate cake? See how he's crying for it!'"

"I've got an aunt like that," the girl replied. Several people laughed. A couple of eyes opened.

"But what does that have to do with *relationships?*" called a green-eyed girl standing at the side of the room.

"Lots," I answered. "False compassion may lead friends to approve of things that aren't right. Or to take sides in conflicts that are none of their business. Or to stay with bad companions. Sometimes it leads someone to take the responsibility to 'make' someone else good. A common kind of false compassion is when a guy or a girl falls for a girl or a guy who's guaranteed bad news. Then there's the kind of false compassion that leads you to give 'help' that doesn't help but only makes *you* feel better. When you indulge your compassionate feelings at the expense of someone else, that's false compassion too."

To my surprise, at each of these examples a hand or a pair of hands went up. By the time I finished, a little grove of hands was waving, and everyone seemed to be awake. Kala looked more hopeful.

"Not so fast," said a guy with glasses that made his eyes like dots. "Could you go over those one at a time?"

"I could if I could remember them," I said.

"Start with the one about falling for wrecked guys," called out the green-eyed young woman. "Lots of girls would like to hear about that one."

"Speak for yourself," called another girl with a grin.

"Hey! Hey! Who are you calling wrecked?" boomed a red-haired guy who reminded me of one of my old college roommates. A ripple of laughter passed among the women in the room, with an answering snicker from the men.

"I see it like this," I said. "Romantic attraction rarely operates by itself. Usually it teams up with other feelings, perhaps unrecognized, and these unrecognized feelings often determine who it is that you're attracted to. Quite a few men and women find themselves attracted mainly to people who are broken in some way. This can happen for a lot of different reasons. One is that you're broken yourself and desperate for someone to love you. But another is plain old sympathy — sympathy draws us to people too, and the sympathetic 'draw' and erotic 'draw' get mixed up together. The upshot is that you fall in love with someone precisely because the person is bad to fall in love with."

Now everyone was paying attention. "So what should you do if you do have that tendency?" asked the guy with strong glasses. "Hypothetically," he added. Laughter again.

"Two things," I said. "One is about you, the other about — in your case — the girl."

"In my *hypothetical* case," he reminded me.

"In your hypothetical case," I agreed. "As to the girl, don't try to play therapist. I don't mean hang her out to dry. Introduce her to Christian girls who have their heads screwed on right and whom you can count on to take her under their wing. As to yourself, don't expect to get therapy from *her*. If you need some straight talk, a good place to start is with a trusted *male* Christian friend."

"That's exactly the opposite of what most people do," said Green-Eyes.

"I know."

"I used to pray with this guy who was a drug addict," she went on. "And the next thing I knew, I'd fallen for him."

"But my dad was a mess when my mom married him," piped up the speak-for-yourself girl. "And she got *him* fixed up."

"I'm not saying it *can't ever work*," I said. "But I'm saying the odds are against it. And what you'll usually find, if you know all the details, is that in those rare cases where it did seem to happen, it *almost didn't* work, worked less well than it *would* have worked if people weren't trying to mix therapy with courtship, and caused a lot of misery in the meantime. Don't do it! Date the kind of person you intend to marry. If you find yourself caring for someone who isn't suitable, the best thing you can do for him is leave him in the hands of Christian friends of the *same* sex until he *becomes* suitable."

"How about one of your other examples?" said the tall fellow who'd spoken first. "You said something about false compassion leading people to take sides."

"Yes," I said. "This one happens mostly among young women, and it has nothing to do with courtship. Most men don't even learn about it until they have teenage daughters, but it continues right into their twenties and thirties. Here's how it happens. Lulu and Marsha have a quarrel. Marsha telephones Susan and sobs out her tale of woe. Susan, full of compassion, sides with Marsha, thinking she's being 'supportive.' But she hasn't heard Lulu's side of the story, and if Lulu had appealed to her first, she probably would have sided with Lulu—not because Lulu has the better case, but because she always sides with *whoever* appeals to her first. If you really want to 'support' your friends, don't take sides in their quarrels at all. Instead, stay on good terms with both—not easy, I know—and encourage them to patch things up."

The red-haired guy broke in. "Taking sides—is that what you meant about false compassion leading people to approve of things that aren't right?"

"No," I said. "There I had something else in mind. Sam and Jock are buddies. Jock is sleeping with his girlfriend. He knows he shouldn't, but he does anyway. She gets pregnant. Jock is afraid and starts thinking about an abortion. He doesn't mention it to his girlfriend yet because he knows abortion is wrong. Instead he talks to Sam. To be a real friend, Sam ought to tell Jock, 'You know you can't do that. Be a stand-up guy. Take care of her. Do the right thing.' Instead, he tries to 'support' Jock by saying, 'I know what you're going through, man. Do what you gotta do.' Unfortunately, that's not true support. It's false compassion. True support is helping your friend be a better man."

"Is that false compassion or false loyalty?" called a guy in the back who looked like a marine.

"With men," I said, "false loyalty is one of the . . ."

"Time!" cried Kala. Her worried look was gone; in fact, she was beaming. "Sorry, but the Q and A has got to stop. Professor Theophilus, lots of people still have questions. Would you come back and speak with us again?"

Like I said, sometimes after you've addressed a group the questions *aren't* about what you've talked about—but that's not necessarily bad. It may give you a clue about what you *should* have talked about.

CHAPTER ELEVEN

NEW, IMPROVED, AND LOWERED STANDARDS

TO SETTLE OR NOT TO SETTLE: IS THAT THE QUESTION?

"Hi, Professor Theophilus!"

I started to call out "Come in," then discovered that she was in already. Instead I said, "Good morning. What can I do for you?"

"You don't remember me, do you?"

"You look familiar. Where have we met?"

"I'm the program chairman for CrossTalk. I wanted to thank you personally for coming back to talk with us again on Monday night. It was a great wind-up for the year, and I was glad to see such a good turnout. Especially since the title, 'Facetious Living,' seemed a little weird before I actually heard what you had to say."

"Yes, of course. I remember you now. Kala, right? Please sit down." I gestured toward a chair. "Didn't my wife and I also meet you at the annual baseball game and picnic—the one where the faculty and administration play against each other?"

"Right. We were introduced by Jordan. I know you know *him* pretty well."

I smiled. "I remember now. He called you his special friend." *Like Brooke,* I thought.

"Jordan calls everyone his special friend. I probably got lost in the crowd." She snickered. "That reminds me. One reason I wanted to thank you personally was that when you talked on Monday about facetious living, you made me realize that I've been living facetiously."

"Oh?"

"Especially in my relationships with guys. I've been wasting time on guys who aren't serious, or who I shouldn't be serious about." She hesitated. "Um, I wonder if I could ask you something about that. You don't have to answer."

"Ask and you shall be answered."

"Thanks. It's not a question *exactly*. But I've been trying to take one of the bits of advice you gave during your talk, and it's turning out harder than I expected."

"What bit?"

"In the 'relationships' part of your talk. You know, how we should lower our standards."

"*Lower* your standards?"

"Isn't that what you said?"

"If anything, I urged *higher* standards."

"You did?"

"Sure. Don't you remember what I said about not dating people who wouldn't be suitable to marry?"

"Yes, but—I guess I'm mixed up. You seemed to say something different during Q and A."

"What did I say during Q and A?"

"A guy spoke up and said he knew that personality is what's really important, but he said physical attraction has to be there too, and his friends told him 'never settle.' I thought you said that wasn't important. Isn't that the same as saying that his standards were too high?"

"Oh, that. I do think people treat looks as too important—but far be it from me to say that it's 'not important' for people looking for marriage partners to be physically attracted to each other."

"Far be it, huh?"

"Right. Humans aren't disembodied spirits. Marriage isn't a purely intellectual enterprise."

"Then since I heard it wrong, what *did* you say to that guy?"

"I probably said that attraction takes time to develop. *Initial* attraction isn't very important."

"But doesn't all attraction start with initial attraction?"

I grinned. "Girl meets guy. Thinks he's good-looking. Gets to know him. Decides he's a creep. Asks herself, 'What did I ever find cute about *him*?'"

"Yea-ah—"

"Hasn't that ever happened to you?"

"Sure, but—"

"How about this one? Girl meets guy. *Doesn't* think he's particularly good-looking. Gets to know him anyway—maybe they have the same friends and keep bumping into each other. Surprisingly, comes to like him. Says to herself, 'Gee, he's a lot cuter than I thought.'"

She pondered. "No, that's never happened to me."

"I see the problem," I laughed. "Your standards aren't too high. You're just in too much of a hurry."

"What do you mean?"

"Attraction and relationship develop together. Maybe it's different in the animal world. There, I suppose, if you look okay, or smell okay, you're in. With us humans, it's the other way around. If you're in, you start looking okay. Even 'physical attraction' isn't purely physical."

"So you're saying that if I meet a guy and he doesn't look like Johnny Drepp, I should give him a chance anyway, because he might look better to me when I get to know him."

"Something like that. Besides, looks go through fashions, just like clothing does. Today, girls think—what was that guy's name?"

"Johnny Drepp."

"Okay, today they think Johnny Drepp is cute. When I was a kid, they thought Sock Hudson was cute."

She made a face and snickered again.

"See what I mean?" I said. "So much of initial attraction is merely a conditioned response. The bell rings, and—"

"And we salivate, like Pavlov's dogs."

"Right. We're just not being serious if we take that too seriously."

"Okay, I get your point. But back up."

"To what?"

"To what you said before. You said that if anything, you encouraged *higher* relationship standards. Not dating people who wouldn't be suitable to marry. Go back to that."

"What about it?"

"I have this friend. She's attracted to guys who wouldn't be suitable to marry. And she's *not* attracted to guys who *would* be. I'm not talking about how they look, but what they're like."

"This friend of yours—does she see this as a problem?"

"Yes and no. I don't—I mean, she doesn't want a bad marriage. But she likes guys to be really male, if you know what I mean."

"I'm not sure whether I do or not. You make being male sound like something bad."

"It is, in a way, isn't it? That kind of guy is always hitting on you. *That's* not good."

"No, but—"

"And he always has an attitude. *That's* not good."

"No, but—"

"And he always has issues with authority. *That's* not good."

"No, but—"

"But that's how really male guys *are*. There's an edge to them. I don't want, I mean, my friend doesn't want a guy who's just a girl with pants on. It's no use telling me, I mean her, 'Don't be attracted to that edge.' That edge is what *makes* them men." Kala's cheeks turned slightly pink. "Anyway, that's what my friend is always saying."

I smiled. "I wasn't going to say, 'Don't be attracted to that edge.'"

"You weren't? Then what were all those 'No, buts' about?"

"Not all edges are the same."

"I don't follow you."

I laughed. "There *is* something edgy about maleness, Kala. Something aggressive, something that pushes, something that wants to be strong. Seeing this, your friend says, 'Given a choice between a guy with an edge and a guy with no edge, I take the guy with an edge.' Am I right so far?"

"Yes. But it scares her."

"That's because she hasn't asked the second question."

"I'll answer for her."

"All right. Let's set aside the guy with no male edge; he's out. But there are different kinds of edges. So we ask, 'Given a choice between a knight's diamond-edged sword and a rusty pocket knife, *this* time which do you take?'"

Kala hedged. "What are you calling a pocket knife and what are you calling a sword?"

"Think of it this way. That edgy male quality has to be sharpened, polished, and oiled, right? As with any good blade."

"I suppose so."

"So much depends on how well the sharpening is done. When the edge turns out well, you get confidence; when it doesn't, you only get attitude. When it turns out well, you get courage and resolution; when it doesn't, you only get moodiness and stubbornness. When it turns out well, you get a man who protects the weak; when it doesn't, you only get a guy who wants to use them."

"You're too late, Professor."

"What do you mean?"

"The women of my generation were raised not to languish in towers, looking for knights on white horses."

"I don't know what you mean by languishing in towers, but I do know this: If you want that male edge, and you run away from knights, you'll end up running after punks."

She hesitated. "You may have something there. But—"

"But what?"

"I don't know any young knights."

I smiled. "At your age, most of them would still be in training. In the middle ages they were called 'squires.'"

"I don't know any squires, either."

"Are you so sure that you'd recognize one if you met him?"

That surprised her. "Why wouldn't I?"

"You're attracted to that male edge. All right, that's natural. You should be. But the right *kind* of edge takes longer to discover. The qualities that are the most obvious are often the most superficial. You have to give a guy a long enough chance to learn what kind of man he really is—and what kind of man he's becoming."

Kala gave an embarrassed little smile. "You say 'you.' Not me. We're talking about my friend. Remember?"

"Of course. But you said that you'd answer for her. Remember?"

She laughed. "I forgot. Thanks, Professor."

COLLEGE RELATIONSHIPS

LETTERS

WORKAHOLIC, FRIENDAPHOBIC

Dear Professor Theophilus:

I'm in an engineering program at a public university. Most people think I have my act together because I've got scholarships, my own apartment, a job after I graduate, and no money worries. Most of my professors know me by name.

But I'm a workaholic. It's getting bad. I'll sleep every other day, and I'm working most of my waking hours. My close friends all have the same major, the same research, and most of the same classes. They aren't Christians. School and work are what we have in common, and that's all we talk about. If I'm not working on a deadline, I'm asleep. I can feel my entire perspective slipping from Christianity to something more like a dog chasing a rabbit. My prayers seem to have fallen to simple SOS calls. I can feel my mentality becoming more like my companions. I only eat when I'm working on something. Like I say, it's getting bad. If I don't set boundaries now, I'll probably have this problem all my life.

In the past I used my parents for balance and for a reality check. I know that Christian friends would be good for me, but honestly, I have little experience with any sort of friendship. Most of my friends before college hung out with me only if I was the only person left in town that they knew. I am incredibly afraid of letting people get close. People may have known me for a year and a half but not know a thing about me. My church and family take it for granted that everyone knows how to make friends or how to react around gals, but I have no idea, especially how to do it in a godly manner. When I ask about "How do Christians interact with people?", no one seems to understand what I mean, and I don't seem to be able to talk about it too well. To top it off, because the kids ridiculed me at church when I was young, I find it harder to trust Christians than non-Christians. In the Bible, most of what I find is nice generic advice that doesn't seem to help someone like me. Especially when there seem to be entire layers of communication I seem to miss.

I don't know if this makes any sense, but if it does, I'd appreciate some advice.

Reply: Thanks for your good letter. I think you're asking three questions: (1) How can you develop friendships? (2) How can you develop normal fellowship with other Christians? and (3) How can you bring your urge to overwork under control? Let's take them in order.

How can you develop friendships? The art of friendship is learned, and it's learned much the same way we learn other things: through practice and perseverance. Just like when you learned to ride a bicycle, you have to be willing to keep trying, even though sometimes you'll fall and get scrapes on your self-regard. Bear in mind that friendship isn't so much a set of "skills" as a set of virtues. At the beginning, for example, you may find it difficult to talk with people whose interests are different than yours, but work at it, because friendship is part of God's design for getting us "outside ourselves." They may feel like "Others," but that's the whole idea. They really aren't you—they're really different people—but they're made, like you, in God's image. Here's a tip: Good friends can give each other a lot of counsel, if they're wise. But in order to give counsel, they have to understand your questions. If I hadn't read your letter, I wouldn't have understood your question "How do Christians interact with people?" either. Make your questions more specific. For example, you could say to a Christian friend, "Tom, you seem to find it easier to talk with girls than I do. How do you get started?"

How can you develop normal fellowship with other Christians? Because you were ridiculed by church kids growing up, this may be hard to believe, but the best place to practice friendship is your Christian student fellowship group. Of course it has to be a reasonably healthy fellowship group, in which the members share not only faith in Christ but lovingkindness toward each other, and in which differences of temperament and gift are appreciated because each person recognizes the others as limbs of the Body of Christ. The sting of ridicule by other kids must have been pretty awful when you were growing up. However, they didn't act like that because they were in church. They acted like that because you were different; children learn how to act by imitation, so they're conformists. The reason they were cruel was that they were too young to have learned how to put themselves in another person's place. So these are limitations of fallen kid-nature, yes, but not of specially church-kid nature. How about the non-Christian study friendships you have now? The reason you don't get hurt in those isn't that they aren't Christian, but that they aren't really friendships, as you admit yourself. You see, by caring for others, we expose ourselves to the risk of pain. The price of never getting hurt is never loving. Here's what I think you need to do. Step one: Spend a few minutes thinking of those church kids who used to ridicule you. Step two: Ask for Christ's help, then take a deep breath and forgive them. In fact, *pray* for them. Step three: Leave the past behind and make a new start on Christian fellowship. There is an ancient saying: *Unus Christianus, nullus Christianus* — "A lone Christian is no Christian."

How can you bring your urge to overwork under control? The answer to this question depends largely on where the urge is coming from. There are a number of possibilities: (1) You're afraid that if you don't overwork, you might fail; (2) Work is a refuge from the burden of social interaction; (3) Work is a distraction from your problems; (4) You seek the respect and approval of your teachers as a substitute for the respect and approval of friends; (5) You don't overwork for any of these reasons, but because of an unexplainable compulsion—as someone else might have a compulsion to repeatedly wash his hands, and another person might have a compulsion to check the door over and over to see if it's really locked.

If the answer is (2), (3), or (4), then as you begin to develop friendships, I think that you will also find it easier to resist the temptation to overwork.

If the answer is (5), then you should seek the assistance of a Christian professional who is skilled in counseling people with obsessions and compulsions.

If the answer is (1), then you need to find out why you are afraid of failure, whether there are any rational grounds for your fear, and what you can do about it. We know you're a good student. Perhaps you are in a field suitable to your talents, but you're merely taking a heavier courseload than necessary. Perhaps your uneasiness arises from the fact that even though you've succeeded in all of your courses, God really intends you for a different field altogether. Or perhaps your fear is irrational, and you should talk to a Christian counselor about how to cope with anxiety. You should also check out the letter "Does It Ever Get Better?" in "Learning to Think Stuff," earlier in this book.

Since you're a good student, I'll give you an assignment. Get into a Christian fellowship group. Attend regularly. With the help of a minister or counselor, draw up a schedule for yourself—one which puts reasonable limits on work, and which also includes time for fellowship, play, and sleep. When you feel the urge to toss the schedule and keep working, say loudly to yourself, "No!"—and follow the schedule anyway. Finally, give thought to the questions and possibilities I raised in the previous paragraphs.

The promise of Jesus is for you, too: "Come to me, all who labor and are heavy laden, and I will give you rest. Take my yoke upon you, and learn from me; for I am gentle and lowly in heart, and you will find rest for your souls. For my yoke is easy, and my burden is light."[15]

Peace be with you,
Professor Theophilus

TRUSTING GOD MEANS TRUSTING BOYFRIEND — TRUE OR FALSE?

Dear Professor Theophilus:

I am engaged to a wonderful Christian man who is a true example of a life redeemed. God gave him His breathtaking beauty in exchange for a mess of ashes. One of the biggest struggles of this relationship is that I've had to decide exactly how much I trust in Christ's work on the Cross. What does it mean that He redeems us? Are we still tainted by our sin, or are we completely cleansed? Does He grudgingly forgive us but still make us suffer for our wrong choices? I've come to realize that I have no room to judge where God has forgiven.

My boyfriend used to be homosexual. For a long time after that, he was still addicted to porn. I already knew that long before we dated. Just recently, though, with great hesitation, he confessed another problem to me — a lengthy struggle with masturbation that had stopped only a short time before we started dating. So many thoughts went through my head. What was it that was so hard to say? How would it affect us? It's hard to hear something like that from someone you love and trust.

But his past doesn't change who he is now. I can forgive the things in his past because I know and trust the man he has become under God's rule.

Reply: I'm so sorry to tell you this, but I can't endorse your judgments. No doubt God has done wonders in your boyfriend's life. Perhaps your boyfriend has even made as much progress as you think. However, you are utterly mistaken in making your ability to believe that this is true a test of your trust in God's grace. It isn't an article of faith that sanctification takes place *all at once.*

Yes, we can be forgiven all in a moment for repented sins, and yes, we can be healed of our sinful propensities. What you are overlooking, however, is that these are not one thing, but two things. "Conversion" is a very different thing than the soul's initial turn to Christ, and the cleansing of our inward sinful tendencies may take a long, long time.

Think of it this way. A soul is like a house. All in a moment, I open the door of my house to Christ, bidding Him to come in. And so He does. Right away He begins scouring, throwing out trash, and letting in light and fresh air. I imagine that I have made Him the Lord of the manor, but have I? Not necessarily. I may only have given Him possession of the entrance hall. After a while—maybe after a very long while—I permit myself to hear His tap-tap-tap on the door of the living room. Reluctantly, I relent and open that door too. He now has possession of both entrance hall and living room. What a relief it is to get them cleaned up. So has He the whole house at last? No, for even now I am shutting Him out of my innermost, secret rooms.

Will I ever allow Him to be truly the Lord of the manor? If I do, how long will it take? For most of us, years, and perhaps with great suffering and struggle. This is *normal.* The suffering is part of the healing, like the pain of dental work.

Something like this has been happening with your young man. First he opened the door to the room of his soul where he had been practicing acts of sodomy. Some time later, he opened the door to the room of his soul where he had been using pornography. Later still, he opened the door to the room of his soul where he had been masturbating. Each time he was forgiven. Is it a test of your faith to believe that there are no locked doors left? No, it is a test of your judgment to weigh the matter carefully. Your young man has relinquished his sexual sins only gradually. The most recent step in this process took place quite recently, after you had already known and trusted him for a long time without having a clue about the problem. What doors has he yet to unlock? Do you know? Are you even in a position to know?

Consider this point too. When a sin is repented and forgiven, the guilt of the sin is gone, cut out, utterly vanished. However, the damage of the sin remains. Already-forgiven sexual sins, for example, may leave not only damage in the body, but deep stains in the imagination and desires, as well as injuries in both the longing and the capacity of the intellect for truth. These stains and injuries generate stronger-than-usual temptations to relapse into the sins themselves. Just as it may take a long time to yield every category of sin to Christ for His forgiveness, so it may take a long time for the Holy Spirit to repair the damage of already-forgiven sin and to heal those preexisting weaknesses which make us susceptible. This too may involve great suffering and struggle.

You haven't asked for advice. Forgive me, but because I am writing for others too, I'll advise you anyway. Not about whether the young man has come far enough to marry—who am I to say yes or no? I can't tell you that, but I can certainly tell you something else. Your duty is not to *believe* that he is marriageable, but to *weigh* whether he is marriageable. To be more careful about him than you have been is not to mistrust Christ's work of redemption—it is to recognize how redemption actually works.

So far, you have been following your feelings about your boyfriend but calling them faith in God. You have been giving yourself a theological excuse *not* to exercise discernment. This has to stop.

Peace be with you,
Professor Theophilus

MISSIONARY SINNING

Dear Professor Theophilus:

I've read Ask Me Anything and a lot of your online articles, so you'd think by this time I'd have this Theophilus thing down. I have a question anyway.

I joined a sorority during my freshman year on the recommendation of two friends I looked up to. They said it was a great way to befriend nonbelievers and lead them to Christ. After a year of sorority life I really have to ask whether I should be immersed in this ungodly environment. Doesn't Psalm 1 say, "Blessed is the man who walks not in the counsel of the wicked"? I'm not tempted to get drunk or have sex, and I do understand the importance of befriending nonbelievers — how else are we to witness to them? But we don't become Muslims to reach Muslims for Christ, do we?

Some Christian friends tell me that I wouldn't be fulfilling God's will if I left the sorority, because I'm here for a reason. What do you think?

Reply: I think your friends' argument begs the question — it assumes what it is supposed to prove. If you're *asking* whether God has a reason for you to be in the sorority, then it doesn't settle anything to say "Don't leave, *because* God has a reason for you to be there." That's what you're trying to find out.

Your own thoughts are much sounder, though I'd use a different analogy. From the way you describe your sorority, hanging out there isn't much like converting to Islam. Observant Muslims aren't big on drunkenness or sluttiness. It's more like living in a bar or brothel. Even though you've stayed chaste and sober, it's not good for you to be there — to live the life of faith you need faithful companions. Nor are you doing any good to your nonbelieving friends — you don't have to join their organization to befriend them, and your witness is compromised by doing so. So I'd advise you to trust your intuitions and get out.

By the way, the line you've been hearing from certain confused Christians is a common one. I call it missionary sinning. Hang out at drug parties—what a chance to spread the Gospel! Date nonbelievers—maybe you can get them to church! Sign up for the wet T-shirt contest—you'll be *such* a witness to the other girls! The general idea seems to be that your witness will be stronger if you weaken it.

Motives for swallowing the line vary. One is pride: "I'm so good that I can expose myself to temptation and *still* not give in." Another is the attraction of sin itself: "I'd like to do these things anyway, but I can't admit that to myself, so I'll just put myself in the path of temptation and wait to give in." You were merely a bit weak with the friends you looked up to; you were afraid to exercise your own judgment and wanted them to think well of you.

I'm glad you've begun to be stronger. Keep it up.

Peace be with you,
Professor Theophilus

MESSING AROUND

Dear Professor Theophilus:

I love a girl I've been dating for two years. We don't have sex, but we often mess around well past our proper limits, and it's getting worse. What can a weak-willed person like me do about this problem?

Reply: Many young Christians assume that when they find themselves in situations which weaken their sexual self-control, they should just stay put and tough it out. That's a huge mistake. Scripture promises help, but it doesn't tell us just to tough out temptation. It tells us to flee it.[16]

Avoiding temptation will require some changes in your relationship, because the first thing an unmarried man and woman need to do is stop spending their time together *alone*. Alone is what you do on your wedding night; that's why it's so cozy. So when you spend time together with your sweetheart, do it where others are present. When you date, go out with a group. When you pray together, have others join you, because prayer is the most intimate time of all. What I'm telling you sounds odd, right? That's because we're no longer used to it. It used to be called common sense.

I've written about the other part of common sense in other places.[17] Do you want to save sex for marriage? Then don't do anything that gets your motor running. God invented sexual arousal to prepare your bodies for sex; did you think it was for something else? And don't think, "We'll do things that arouse us, but we won't cross that line." That's like turning on powerful rocket motors, but saying "Don't lift off." If sex is for marriage, sexual arousal must be too.

Peace be with you,
Professor Theophilus

BORED ON BREAK

Dear Professor Theophilus:

Do you have any practical advice for college students who go home on college holidays and breaks? On campus, there is always class to attend, people to meet, work to do — all these are opportunities for ministry. But at home during break, I don't do much, except for church twice a week. It's all too easy to lounge around all day, sleep in, and watch TV, even though that's obviously unsatisfactory. A complication in my own case is that my family has moved to a part of the country new to me. At the new church, the people closest to my age are a lot younger, and in the new neighborhood, I won't have anyone I can hang out with.

I want to make the best of my time, but breaks can be up to three weeks long. Other than reading my Bible and praying daily, how can I make the most of the time I have off from school? Help!

Reply: The funny thing about your letter is that after asking a great question, you come close to ruling out my answer. *Other than* prayer and meditation, you ask, what can you do? What I want to answer is, *why not* pray and meditate? Why not think of your school break as your own personal spiritual retreat?

I know the idea seems crazy. One thing that makes it seem crazy is childhood habit. When we were small, our parents taught us quick morning and evening prayers like "Now I lay me down to sleep, I pray the Lord my soul to keep," just to introduce us to the idea of praying to God. Even though we may have learned adult forms of prayer since then, the idea persists that prayer and spiritual reading are things that we do for a little while at special times, then finish. It seems unimaginable to "pray without ceasing," as St. Paul urges.

Another reason is that some of the forms of prayer that we've learned as adults are themselves too limited. For example, we may think that prayer is all talking. Sure, there are lots of things to talk about—we praise God, we thank Him, we confess our sins, we intercede for other people, we ask Him for what we need—but pretty soon we run out of things to say.

My suggestion, then, is twofold. First, learn more about the riches of Christian traditions of prayer and meditation. You can even link your prayer to the Christian calendar. For example, during the days leading up to Easter you can try the spiritual exercise called the Stations of the Cross. There are both Protestant and Catholic versions of this exercise, but the basic elements are the same in both: One by one, you meditate prayerfully on each of the events leading up to and including the Crucifixion. First comes the condemnation of Jesus to death, next the carrying of the Cross, next when He falls the first time, and so on. Or you might try the spiritual exercise called *lectio divina*. The idea is to read a passage of Scripture—but slowly, thoughtfully, as a prayer. Which passage? Still supposing that you're home for Easter break, you can start with the Passion story. In Matthew, for example, that's in chapters 26–27; you can save chapter 28 for Easter morning. One of the great things about this kind of prayer is that it's not all about us. It's all about Him.

Second, for those times that you *aren't* praying and meditating, do something useful. Offer the work to Christ while you're doing it, so that the work itself becomes a form of prayer. I'm not talking about paid employment. Not many employers would want to hire you for only a few days or weeks anyway. The place to start looking is your home. Take over one of the family responsibilities! What's stopping you from, say, making all the family meals during your break from school? And yes, I said "making," not "helping"! In the time left over from that, what's keeping you from volunteering to make sandwiches every morning in the downtown Christian ministry to street people? The traditional Christian way to use spare time is in works of love. I guarantee that you won't have time to be bored.

How fortunate you are that because you're still in college, you can go on a personal spiritual retreat every break and every holiday! Thousands of graduates would beg for a chance like that.

Peace be with you,
Professor Theophilus

TRYING TO FIX HIM

Dear Professor Theophilus:

My boyfriend and I have been dating for nine months, and since the beginning we have been pretty physical. Finally I decided that this was hurting my relationship with God too much, so I set sharp limits. What you've written about premarital sex helped me know where to set them. My problem is that my boyfriend is not a virgin and sees nothing wrong with sex or anything else before marriage. He won't stop pestering me to change my mind and relent on my limits. The easy answer would be to break up, right? Well, I really don't want to do that. He's got a lot of emotional problems, and I don't want to add to them, since he really does care for me.

Reply: I don't see why you say the fellow cares for you—he may have strong feelings, but the strongest seems to be "I want my way." He proves this not only by nagging you for sex, but also by using his emotional problems to keep you under control.

I'm also concerned about you because compassion is one of the worst possible reasons to date a man. A girlfriend is not a counselor. You won't "fix" the guy; you'll only break yourself.

The fact that you make excuses for your boyfriend instead of realistically appraising his character is a serious danger sign. The fact that you say, "I know what to do, but please tell me something else," is another.

Peace be with you,
Professor Theophilus

JUST LIKE A BROTHER

Dear Professor Theophilus:

I'm in a long-distance relationship, and my boyfriend wants to come over for a week during his school break. He says he wants to stay in my apartment, because he doesn't know anyone else here and can't afford a hotel. We're both Christians, and he promised that we wouldn't fall into sin. He said he would be just like a brother.

When I told him that I wasn't comfortable with this plan, he became very hurt, said I didn't trust him, and told me I'm being selfish. He said that he wouldn't come again.

I feel really bad because I like him a lot and I didn't want to hurt him. What do I do?

Reply: He says *he's* hurt? What an understanding guy. Good for you for hanging tough, and shame on him for trying to "guilt you" into doing something wrong.

"You shall not tempt the Lord your God."[18] To room together yet expect God to protect you from falling into sin would have been like throwing yourselves from a building yet expecting God to keep you from hitting the ground. We are under strict command from the Lord to flee not only from sin, but from temptation. What your boyfriend means by "trusting him" is believing that he's above temptation, but no human being is above temptation.

You ask what you can do. You've done it, my dear. Don't think you can patch up the relationship by giving in. It's up to him to respect the boundary you've set, and if he doesn't, you need to tell him good-bye. The fact that you *do* feel guilty for doing the right thing suggests that you need to be stronger.

Peace be with you,
Professor Theophilus

DID WE BREAK UP OR DIDN'T WE?

Dear Professor Theophilus:

Recently, my boyfriend and I broke up. At first, things weren't so serious — we were just testing it out in a way, trying to see if more would develop. Things were getting physical, and the things he said to me made me feel wonderful. I really liked him a lot! It ended very suddenly when I found out that he cared for me only "a little more than friendship."

Was I ever upset! I'd opened my heart up, I'd fallen in love with his family, and for the first time in a relationship I felt able to be myself. We broke off because I didn't feel I could continue being physical when he didn't care about me as more than a friend. I'm so hurt now, and I'm afraid that guys will trick me into thinking they care for me when they really don't. I never thought a friend would do that to me!

He still wants to be friends, and I think — it is possible. However, I don't think things can ever be the same! Should I talk to him about how I feel and how he hurt me? Or should I just let it go?

Reply: When you break up, break up; "still being friends" is an illusion in two different ways. First, it makes the situation ambiguous; you've broken up, but somehow you haven't broken up. Second, there isn't any "still" in a case like yours because you weren't the friends that you thought you were in the first place. A friend wouldn't have used you merely for sexual recreation.

Should you talk with the man and tell him how you feel about how he used you? The time to tell him was when you broke up with him, and that opportunity has passed. So let it go. The important thing now isn't telling him how you feel, but learning from what happened — and the biggest lesson to learn is that what you call "getting physical" isn't an appropriate activity for a date, no matter how wonderful the things the guy says make you feel.

The correct term for "getting physical" is "foreplay," and the right time for it is your wedding night, when you are preparing to consummate your marriage. If you use it as a way to feel good about guys, then guys will use you to feel good. That is neither a good way to find a suitable man, nor a good way to become a suitable woman.

Peace be with you,
Professor Theophilus

FLEEING FROM
GOD STUFF

WHAT THIS SECTION IS ABOUT

St. Augustine wrote, "Thou hast made us for Thyself and our hearts are restless till they rest in Thee."[19] Everyone is fleeing either toward that rest or from it.

We like to think this isn't true, that we can just drift or stand still. That is one of the great illusions of the human race. What looks like drifting is actually another way to run. What looks like standing still is one of the fastest ways to flee. If you haven't noticed that before, you might in college.

This section is about fleeing from God, about thinking of fleeing from Him, and about thinking of turning around and fleeing home. Anyone considering the third alternative should remember that although the way back home is long in one way, it's short in another, because Christ is not only the Destination. He is also the Road.

CHAPTER FOURTEEN

AS THOUGH THERE WERE NO GOD

WHY BEING AGNOSTIC ISN'T THE SAME AS BEING UNCOMMITTED

Class had been over for only ten minutes when Nathan turned up at my office door, saying, "I brought your coffee mug back."

"What? Good morning. I didn't even know you had it."

"I didn't," he declared. "You left it behind in class again." He put it in my hand.

"Oh, no. Did you come all the way up here just to return it? Thank you."

"It's okay. I was coming anyway."

"Then sit," I said, gesturing.

He did, but tentatively, like a bird on the end of a twig. "I wasn't sure if my question is office hours material," he said. "It's about something you said in class."

"Why shouldn't that be office hours material?"

"Because actually my question is personal."

I spread my hands. "Ask."

"This morning someone asked a question about all that 'Creator' language in the Declaration of Independence."

"I remember."

"You said something about a French guy who influenced the thinking of the American Founders. Burly or Burlap or something. There's a 'key' in it."

"Burlamaqui."

"That's him. You said he made a big deal about God. I wasn't too interested. I hadn't had my coffee yet, you know? Then you got my attention."

"How?"

"Well, you didn't say flat out whether you think there *is* a God. But you said you thought this Burlamaqui guy was right to make a big deal about the question. Here's what I want to know."

"I'm listening."

"What does it matter?"

I was a bit puzzled. "Nathan, it sounds like you're asking, 'Why is it important to know about the Most Important Thing?'"

"I think I'm asking why it *is* the Most Important Thing."

"Perhaps it would help you to think of the other questions you consider important."

"Like what?"

"Whether to live. How to live. Whether there is anything to live for. What life means. The God question makes a difference to *all* those questions."

"What do you mean when you say it 'makes a difference' to them?"

"If there is a God, the answers come out one way; if there isn't, they come out another. It also makes a difference what kind of God He is."

"But we can't know whether God is real anyway."

I lifted a quizzical eyebrow. "How do you know we can't know?"

He shrugged. "I take it back. I don't know we can't know. But I know *I* don't know."

"Have you tried to find out?"

"Uh-huh. During my sophomore year."

"Tell me about that."

"I was sort of obsessed. I read so many books and talked with so many people about whether there's a God that I was losing sleep and making myself sick. So please don't tell me to read another book, and please don't ask me, 'Have you considered this argument?'"

I laughed. "Whatever you say."

"So now I just say I'm agnostic."

"What do you mean by that?"

"I mean I don't say there is a God, and I don't say there isn't one," he answered. "I'm not committed either way."

I was still holding the mug Nathan had returned. "You said you hadn't had your coffee," I said, standing. "I'm going to make some; would you like a cup?" That would give me time to think.

"I'd love one," he answered, surprised. "But I didn't bring anything to drink from."

"Look on the bookshelf behind you." After Nathan had fetched one of the cups and seated himself again, he seemed more relaxed.

I measured out the water from a carafe, counted out the scoops, and flipped the switch. Shortly the coffee maker was emitting little pops and chuckles. It always makes me think of a hen. When I had poured out two cups I turned back to Nathan.

"So you don't believe in God."

"I don't believe in Him and I don't *dis*believe in Him. Like I said, I'm agnostic."

"What would you say if I told you that in a certain way, I don't believe in agnostics?"

Not sure whether I was joking, he made a little laugh. "But I exist," he said. "You see me. Here I am."

I smiled back and sipped my coffee. "I believe that you exist. And I believe that you don't know what to think. But you said an agnostic is 'not committed either way,' and I don't believe that there is such a thing as 'not committed either way.'"

He shook his head. "If I don't *know* the answer to the God question, then how could I be *committed* to an answer to the God question?"

"Commitments are reflected in movements of the will."

"What does that mean?"

"They're reflected in how we live."

"So which answer to the God question am I committed to by how I live?"

"Oh, I haven't any idea."

"But I thought you meant—"

"Why, no. Answering that question would require me to have personal knowledge about you that I don't possess."

"You mean you'd have to ask questions about my life?"

I laughed again. "I'm not proposing to ask you questions about your life, Nathan. I'm just your teacher."

"That's okay. I came here with a personal question, not a course question. This is related."

"That's true," I conceded.

"So are you saying that if you *did* ask me questions about my life, then you *could* tell me what answer to the God question I'm committed to?"

"Possibly."

"Then do it. I want to know."

I hesitated. "All right. You asked for it. Do you pray?"

"I used to sometimes, but I stopped. Seemed kind of pointless, since I didn't know whether anyone was listening."

"Do you have plans for the future?"

"I'll probably go to law school. There's always work for lawyers. They make pretty good money, and I think I'd like the work okay."

"What do you aim for in life?"

"Not getting bored. Having enough money to buy the things that I want. Not working *all* the time. Having fun."

"Will you get married? Have kids?"

"I'm okay with my sex life as it is. If it gets old someday, then maybe I'll settle down. Kids, I don't know. That seems like a pretty big interruption in my life. But hey," Nathan added, "this isn't too bad. How am I doing?"

I smiled. "No more questions."

He smiled back lopsidedly. "Sorry my answers were so uninformative."

"What makes you think they were uninformative?"

"They didn't reveal a 'commitment' like you were expecting."

"On the contrary."

"You mean they did?"

"Of course they did. Nathan, there is no such thing as neutrality. Every way of life is *some* way of life. Inevitably, you live either as though there were a God, or as though there weren't. You stake your life on an answer you say you don't have."

"So which answer am I staking my life on?"

"Consider my question about whether you pray. You say you don't know whether anyone is at the other end listening. But if you're really not sure, then why not say, 'I'll pray, because maybe there is'? Instead you say, 'I won't, because maybe there *isn't.*' That makes sense only if it's really true that there isn't."

He paused. Light dawned. "Yeah, I see that."

"Or consider my questions about your future. You say you don't know whether God is real. But if you're really not sure, then in planning your future, why not ask, 'What use *might* a good God have for my gifts?' Instead you consult only your pleasure. Even if the meaning of happiness is merely pleasure—which, by the way, it isn't—that makes sense only if you can be sure that no such God *does* take an interest."

"I guess that's right too."

"Or take those questions about marriage. Marriage is either about the total gift of yourself to your spouse, or about personal sexual convenience. The former way of viewing it makes sense if a self-giving God created it; the latter way makes sense if only He didn't. You didn't give the former way a single thought."

"That's true. I see where you're going."

"Where?"

"You're saying that I live—as though there were no God."

"Right. You say you're uncommitted, but in practice you're committed to atheism."

Nathan was unperturbed. "But Prof, since I *don't* know the answer to the God question, how else *can* I live?"

I answered, "Instead of living as though there were no God, you could try living as though there were."

That was when the other shoe dropped. His face turned ashen. "You mean—like pray?"

"That, and other things. Seek His will and follow it."

"How can I seek what might not be there?"

"If you did seek it, you might find out."

There was a long, long pause. I had spoken the Abominable Thought. A look of infinite dismay spread over Nathan's face. One could have read the signs from ten feet away; as his mental censors crumbled, an awful question was welling slowly up from the base of his mind.

If only he did seek it, he might find out. He saw that now.

But did he really want to find out?

CHAPTER FIFTEEN

NOT MUCH USE FOR GOD

WHEN PEOPLE RUN FROM GOD IT'S NOT USUALLY BECAUSE THEY DON'T BELIEVE IN HIM.

To: *m.e.theophilus@posteverything.state.edu*
From: *rachel@sullen.com*
Subject: *question*

Hi, Professor Theophilus. I was wondering whether you'd finished assigning grades for the Civilization course. It's a big class, so maybe you don't remember me. I'm the girl at the end of the third row who fell asleep during the final exam, and I've been a little worried about how I did. Also I might have another question. Thanks, Rachel

To: *rachel@sullen.com*
From: *m.e.theophilus@posteverything.state.edu*
Subject: *re: question*

Dear Rachel: I gave your final exam a B–, which earned you a straight B for the course. Pretty good, considering that you slept through questions five and six. I hope you haven't been ill. What's your other question? Sincerely, Professor Theophilus

To: m.e.theophilus@posteverything.state.edu
From: rachel@sullen.com
Subject: other question

Dear Professor Theophilus: That's a relief. I thought I might have bombed the exam. No, I'm not sick. It's just that a lot has been going on and I didn't get much sleep during finals week. My question is about the Q and A after your final lecture. A guy in the front row asked a question about the Job reading and your answer quoted a religious policeman. What was it that you said? Thanks, Rachel

To: rachel@sullen.com
From: m.e.theophilus@posteverything.state.edu
Subject: re: other question

Dear Rachel: You'll have to help me out here, because I remember several questions about the reading selection from the book of Job, but I don't remember saying anything like that. Are you sure it was a religious policeman? Sincerely, Professor Theophilus

To: m.e.theophilus@posteverything.state.edu
From: rachel@sullen.com
Subject: religious policeman

Dear Professor Theophilus: Could he have been a detective? Anyway, he was religious, and he said something about a tapestry. Thanks, Rachel

To: rachel@sullen.com
From: m.e.theophilus@posteverything.state.edu
Subject: re: religious policeman

Dear Rachel: I understand now. The famous journalist and Christian apologist G. K. Chesterton wrote a series of stories and novels about a priest named Father Brown, who was also an amateur detective. In "The Sins of Prince Saradine," the characters are discussing the mystery of injustice and unpunished evil, and one of them asks Father Brown whether he believes in "doom," meaning fate. Father Brown says no, he believes in "Doomsday," meaning the day of judgment. Because the other fellow doesn't understand, he tells him what he means: "I mean that we here are on the wrong side of the tapestry," answered Father Brown. "The things that happen here do not seem to mean anything; they mean something somewhere else. Somewhere else retribution will come on the real offender. Here it often seems to fall on the wrong person."[20] In class I might have stated the lines inaccurately because I was quoting from memory. Is this what you were asking about? Sincerely, Professor Theophilus

To: m.e.theophilus@posteverything.state.edu
From: rachel@sullen.com
Subject: re: re: religious policeman

Dear Professor Theophilus: Yes, that was the quotation, thanks. I wish I could believe it. Rachel

To: rachel@sullen.com
From: m.e.theophilus@posteverything.state.edu
Subject: "wish I could believe it"

Dear Rachel: Do you want to discuss it? Sincerely, Professor T

To: m.e.theophilus@posteverything.state.edu
From: rachel@sullen.com
Subject: re: "wish I could believe it"

Dear Professor Theophilus: I don't know. I guess I must, because I asked you about it. But my father died last year, my brother just announced that he's gay, my other brother is all messed up on drugs, and none of this looks like Eternal Justice to me. I don't have much use for God right now. Rachel

To: rachel@sullen.com
From: m.e.theophilus@posteverything.state.edu
Subject: re: re: "wish I could believe it"

Dear Rachel: What do you want Him to do? Professor T

To: m.e.theophilus@posteverything.state.edu
From: rachel@sullen.com
Subject: obvious

Dear Professor Theophilus: Isn't that obvious? I want Him to change my brothers and bring my father back to life. And if He can't or won't do that, I want Him to leave me alone. Please tell me what you really think, not what you're supposed to say as a professor. I've got my grades and I'm graduating anyway. Rachel

To: *rachel@sullen.com*
From: *m.e.theophilus@posteverything.state.edu*
Subject: *what I really think*

Dear Rachel: What I really think is that you're right—a God who couldn't change your brothers and bring your father back to life would hardly be worth the name. But the God I worship does change people; He brings all the dead back to life, whether to unending joy or unending sorrow; and I don't think you would ask Him to leave you alone if you knew what you were asking. Getting one's way on that point is the condition we call hell. Professor T

To: *m.e.theophilus@posteverything.state.edu*
From: *rachel@sullen.com*
Subject: *excuses*

Dear Professor Theophilus: Then that must be where I am, because He sure is leaving me alone. I'd expected you to make excuses for Him. Rachel

To: *rachel@sullen.com*
From: *m.e.theophilus@posteverything.state.edu*
Subject: *re: excuses*

Dear Rachel: No, a God who takes upon Himself the death that we deserve doesn't need me to make excuses for Him. But I don't think He has really left you alone. That would be much worse. Professor T

To: *m.e.theophilus@posteverything.state.edu*
From: *rachel@sullen.com*
Subject: *where then?*

Dear Professor Theophilus: If He hasn't left me alone, then where is He? He must have an odd way of making His presence known. Rachel

To: *rachel@sullen.com*
From: *m.e.theophilus@posteverything.state.edu*
Subject: *re: where then?*

Dear Rachel: Not so odd. He has sent messengers to you and provoked you to ask them for news of Him. Professor T

To: *m.e.theophilus@posteverything.state.edu*
From: *rachel@sullen.com*
Subject: *re: re: where then?*

Dear Professor Theophilus: That statement strikes me as even odder. I haven't met anyone lately with a halo or wings, and I certainly haven't had any conversations with such a person. Rachel

To: *rachel@sullen.com*
From: *m.e.theophilus@posteverything.state.edu*
Subject: *re: re: re: where then?*

Dear Rachel: Not that kind of messenger. People. What do you call the conversation we're having now? If you didn't notice that I was bringing news, it's not surprising that you haven't recognized other newsbringers. That doesn't mean there haven't been any. Professor T

To: m.e.theophilus@posteverything.state.edu
From: rachel@sullen.com
Subject: mother

Dear Professor Theophilus: My mother has been after me about going back to church. I got really angry with her one day because she's not angry enough about my father dying. When she's sad she sings the Psalms. It really burns me. I suppose you would consider her another messenger. Rachel

To: rachel@sullen.com
From: m.e.theophilus@posteverything.state.edu
Subject: re: mother

Dear Rachel: It seems likely. She comes from the place of solace to tell you that you don't need to be angry, but you're angry because she comes from the place of solace. Is it possible that you've got it turned around? Professor T

To: m.e.theophilus@posteverything.state.edu
From: rachel@sullen.com
Subject: brothers

Dear Professor Theophilus: What about my brothers? Rachel

To: rachel@sullen.com
From: m.e.theophilus@posteverything.state.edu
Subject: re: brothers

Dear Rachel: What about them? Professor T

To: *m.e.theophilus@posteverything.state.edu*
From: *rachel@sullen.com*
Subject: *re: re: brothers*

Dear Professor Theophilus: I told you. One has decided that he's gay, and let me tell you, his life isn't "gay" in the "happy" sense at all. The other is all messed up on drugs. Are they messengers too? Rachel

To: *rachel@sullen.com*
From: *m.e.theophilus@posteverything.state.edu*
Subject: *re: re: re: brothers*

Dear Rachel: No. But they might be messages. "This is what happens when you tell God to leave you alone." How much do you want God to change them, Rachel? Professor T

To: *m.e.theophilus@posteverything.state.edu*
From: *rachel@sullen.com*
Subject: *how much?????*

Dear Professor Theophilus: What kind of question is that????? Rachel

To: *rachel@sullen.com*
From: *m.e.theophilus@posteverything.state.edu*
Subject: *re: how much?????*

Dear Rachel: I asked because God may already have a plan to change them, but it may cost more than you're willing to spend. I don't mean money. Professor T

To: m.e.theophilus@posteverything.state.edu
From: rachel@sullen.com
Subject: re: re: how much?????

Dear Professor Theophilus: What do you mean? Rachel

To: rachel@sullen.com
From: m.e.theophilus@posteverything.state.edu
Subject: re: re: re: how much?????

Dear Rachel: What if God, in His sovereign mercy, has chosen *you* as the instrument of His grace to your brothers? What if you're the only messenger He can send to *them* about Himself? Professor T

To: m.e.theophilus@posteverything.state.edu
From: rachel@sullen.com
Subject: don't get it

Dear Professor Theophilus: I don't get it. Explain. Rachel

To: rachel@sullen.com
From: m.e.theophilus@posteverything.state.edu
Subject: re: don't get it

Dear Rachel: If God has no one else to send to your brothers, then your unwillingness to be reconciled with Him because He hasn't changed your brothers might be the very thing that keeps Him from changing them. If He wants to use you that way, then you might have to let go of your anger against Him before He can do anything about the things that are making you angry. That's why I say His plan may cost more than you're willing to spend. Professor T

To: *m.e.theophilus@posteverything.state.edu*
From: *rachel@sullen.com*
Subject: *how much I'm willing to spend*

Dear Professor Theophilus: So you're saying that I have to decide whether it's more important to me to see my brothers change, or to stay angry with God because they haven't. Rachel

To: *rachel@sullen.com*
From: *m.e.theophilus@posteverything.state.edu*
Subject: *re: how much I'm willing to spend*

Dear Rachel: Now you've got it. What do you think you'll do? Professor T

CHAPTER SIXTEEN

THE FAILURE OF THEOPHILUS

ANOTHER WAY OF RUNNING AWAY FROM GOD

I haven't seen Clay for years, but despite my poor memory for names and faces I'm not likely to forget him. Late twenties, returned college dropout, determined to do better the second time around. Comfortable with friends, uncomfortable with classmates. Heavy guy. Slight limp. Looked like he'd had some hard knocks. Spoke apologetically but intelligently in class. Quiet voice with gravelly edges.

I liked him. He was also my greatest failure. We were two weeks into the semester when he showed up at my office.

"Professor, I gotta talk with you."

I waved him in, wondering at the melodrama. "What do we gotta talk about?"

He sat down on the chair in the corner, by my desk. "I gotta tell you that I'm getting scared."

Was he putting me on? I asked, "Why are you getting scared?"

"Because you're scaring me. See? I'm shaking."

He held out his hand, and sure enough, it was trembling. There are lots of things that can cause a hand to tremble. I could picture Clay shaking from a hangover or from not enough sleep. But he said that he was scared.

"How am I scaring you?"

He replied, "It's Aristotle."

"How is Aristotle scaring you?"

"In this book of his you made us read he keeps talking about virtue."

I lifted an eyebrow. "So?"

"It's making me realize that I haven't led a virtuous life."

As I realized that he was on the level, the truth of the moment sank into me. But you have to know something about Aristotle to understand what passed through my mind.

Wisest of the pagans, Aristotle did teach about virtue. Without courage, justice, frankness, self-control, and all the rest of the moral excellences, he said, no one can be happy in the full sense of the term. If you hadn't led a virtuous life and weren't happy, and then you read Aristotle and realized that he was right, you might well be depressed about all the years that you had wasted.

But you wouldn't be *afraid*. Aristotle would merely tell you to start learning virtue. As wise as a pagan could be, yet he knew nothing about "working out your salvation in fear and trembling." For all his wisdom in other matters, he didn't know grace from a hatstand.

Could I have been the cause of Clay's fear? Scripture says the fear of the Lord is the beginning of wisdom. I do tell my students that I'm Christian; it's my custom to make mention of the fact on the first day of the semester because they ought to know where their teachers are coming from. That's simple honesty. But this semester I hadn't said a word about my faith. On the first day, I had just forgotten, and another suitable moment had never come.

So it seemed that Clay was right. The trigger for his fear wasn't my faith, and it wasn't me. It was Aristotle. This amazed me. The Gospel of John teaches that the Holy Spirit came to bring the world conviction of guilt concerning sin and righteousness and judgment—but I had never thought He might use a pagan to do it.

Around this time I began to tremble myself. Not in my hands. In my heart.

Clay was waiting for an answer. I hesitated. He wasn't a former student; he was under my authority *now*, this very semester, in this very course. I had to be sure that he wouldn't feel pressure to agree with me just because I was his teacher.

"Are you asking me how Aristotle would advise you to live?"

"No. I understand that. I'm telling you that I'm scared."

"I can speak about that, but not as your teacher. I can only do it from the perspective of my faith."

"Would you do that?"

"Are you giving me permission to speak man-to-man?"

"Yes. That's what I want you to do."

"All right. Look." I made as though I were lifting something from my head. "I'm taking off my professor hat. Nothing I say here represents Post Everything University. Nothing you say here affects your standing in the course. You're free to say anything you want."

"I want you to speak from your faith."

I looked at him a moment longer. "Clay, I think you're experiencing what the New Testament calls the conviction of sin."

He took in a breath and let it out. "That must be it."

"Because I said so?"

"No, because it fits. You don't have any idea. I've done a lot of bad things."

"Everyone has. Paul says, 'All men sin and fall short of the glory of God.'"

"Not like me."

"Just like you. Has anyone ever explained the Gospel to you?"

"I don't think so."

"Gospel means Good News. The Gospel is the message of Christianity. The Bad News you know already—that's why you're scared. We make a mess of things. It's not God's fault—He didn't make us that way—but we've been rebelling against Him from the beginning. We're guilty, and we're broken."

"That's the Bad News?"

"That and one other thing. We can't forgive ourselves, and we can't fix ourselves."

"I do know that. What's the Good News?"

"God offers to forgive us and fix us and bring us back to Himself. He can do this because He's taken the heat for us already. That's what the Cross is all about."

"I know that Jesus died on the Cross and that He was supposed to have risen again, but I never understood why."

"When Jesus was suffering on the Cross, He was taking the burden of our brokenness, our guilt, and our separation from God on Himself. That's why I said He took the heat for us. And then He arose from death to new life. Do you understand?"

"Yes," Clay said simply. A little surprised, I went on.

"The Gospel—the Good News—is that if we believe what He did and entrust our whole selves and lives to Him as Savior and Lord—that means as Rescuer and Boss—then in some way, what He did counts just as though we had done it ourselves. He died on the Cross, and we die to our sinful selves through Him. He rose again, and we rise to a new life through Him. So if we turn to Him—I'm not saying there isn't a lot of blood, sweat, and tears, but there is also grace—we don't have to be scared anymore."

I paused. "Do you believe all this?"

Clay said, "Yes."

Dear God, I thought, *the fruit is ripe and dropping off the tree.*

I asked, "Then do you understand what you have to do?"

"Yes."

"Do you want to do it?"

After a few moments of silence, Clay said, "No."

Inwardly I was staggered. How could you believe it and not want to do it? The words of James came back to me: "Even the demons believe—and shudder."[21]

"Why don't you, Clay?"

"I believe what you said, Professor Theophilus. But God couldn't forgive *me*."

"How are you different than other people?"

"You don't know what I've done."

"There is nothing God can't forgive, if only the person turns away from what he has done and turns to Christ instead."

"Professor Theophilus, that's easy for you to say. You say it because you haven't lived the way I have. You're a good man."

"That's not true. On my own I'm a sinful man. If you see good in me, I thank God for it, but it's only because the power of Christ has been healing me. I may not sin so often or so obviously as I used to, but you didn't know me before I knew Him, and you don't really know me now."

"No, you're a good man," he persisted. "You're probably married and have kids."

I conceded that this was true.

"I just live with a woman," he said.

"Jesus forgave thieves and prostitutes," I said.

His voice dropped to a murmur. "But there have been—abortions. And other things."

"I was a wreck before turning to Christ," I replied. "Just through my teaching, I'm probably responsible for more abortions than you are. If I can be forgiven, you can."

"No. I'm not good enough to be forgiven."

I saw that he was leading me in circles. This was when I should have prayed for help, but I didn't. Instead I tried to redirect the conversation myself. I said good things. They just weren't the right ones.

"When you say that," I asked, "aren't you missing the *point* of forgiveness?"

"How?"

"It's *because* we aren't good enough that we need to be forgiven in the first place. The idea of being good enough to be forgiven gets it backward. Forgiveness can't be earned."

"You mean it's like a gift?"

"I mean it *is* a gift."

He chewed on the idea. "I see that," he said, "but I'm too bad to be forgiven. God can forgive other people, but I'm beyond the limit."

"Clay," I said, "there's something fishy here. You want me to think that God's standards are too high for you, and it's true that we don't reach them; that's why we need His forgiveness. But when you say you're too sinful to be forgiven, aren't you really saying that God's standards are *too low* for you?"

"What do you mean?"

"I mean He's willing to forgive you, but you won't let Him — as though your standards were higher than His. Believe me, Clay, you can't be more holy than God is."

He said nothing.

"Besides, God Himself says He is ready to forgive you. You said a few minutes ago that you believed it. Have you changed your mind already?"

"No. But I'm different. He didn't mean me."

I shot my last bolt. "This idea of yours that everyone can be forgiven except you — isn't it just pride? It's as though you were the King of Sinners, as though your power to sin were greater than His power to forgive. He paid the ultimate price, but for you alone it wasn't enough. Do you see what an insult that is to Him?"

Finally Clay spoke, but only to return to an earlier point in the conversation. "I'm not virtuous like you are, Professor Theophilus. God can't forgive me."

I knew he was stonewalling. I think he knew it too. We spoke for a few minutes more. He thanked me for talking with him, then left.

That was fourteen years ago. I used to bump into him around campus. We'd always stop and chat, but not about God.

I know what I should have said to him that day. In prayer afterward, God made it obvious to me. Being too sinful to be forgiven was just Clay's pretense. He didn't really think he couldn't be forgiven; the real issue was that he didn't want to be. It would have required giving up his sins. It would have required allowing God to change him. It would have required cooperating with His grace.

But I should have been having that prayer while the conversation was still going on.

I've learned to be a more prayerful witness. And God has forgiven me. But I pray that He will stir up Clay to seek a better witness than I was to him.

I wonder whether Clay still uses his guilt as a barrier against unwanted mercy. I wonder if he still finds security in being scared.

And I ask God to show him the grace that He once showed me.

FLEEING FROM GOD

LETTERS

HE'S NOT THE BOSS OF ME

Dear Professor Theophilus:

You say that God is good, but what makes Him good? You say that we have been ruined by trying to be good without God, but by whose standard? God's? Of course if we break away from Him we will be ruined by His standard, but what makes His standard better than yours, mine, or my cat's? All I really want to know is what makes this being better and more morally right.

Reply: Your mistake is thinking of God as something separate from Good—He may be in accord with it, He may not. That's not how it is. God and Good aren't two things; they are one. He simply *is* the Good, and good things short of Him are good because He made them. It's His goodness that these thousand goods reflect, as white light refracted through a prism gleams in a thousand brilliant colors—love, joy, wisdom, beauty, strength, and all the rest. Now think hard: God cannot be at odds with Himself. It is because He *is* the Good, and with infinite wisdom knows Himself, that He knows what Good is. So to think that you, or I, or your cat might know Good better than Good knows Himself is pretty silly.

Another way to answer was suggested by C. S. Lewis.[22] God is the source of our ability to know about Good. In that sense you could

say His standard *is* our standard. He gave us our minds and our conscience. He was the one who made us able to see that evil and good
are *different*, who polarized our souls to fear the one and long for the
other. The very power to ask questions and form judgments about the
matter comes from Him and depends on Him. So to set this power
against Him is like sawing off the branch that we are sitting on.

That answers your question; in fact it answers it twice. But here
is something else to think about. Christ, whose coming was promised from ancient times, has been called the Desire of Nations.[23] The
reason for this title is that if He Himself is the Good, then whether
or not we know it, to long for the Good is ultimately to long for Him.
Turning the same thought around, to seek good things *apart* from
the One from whom their goodness comes is ultimately to stuff our
mouths with dust and ashes. There will come a day when you wonder
why you can't swallow. Come to the Fountain instead.

Peace be with you,
Professor Theophilus

EMPTINESS IN CHRIST?

Dear Professor Theophilus:

*I am a Witch and I follow the Wiccan path. It always amazes me when I read
things like yours. You Christians pretend that your religion is correct. You show
your intolerance for others by attacking other religions. You cannot conceive that
people would be happy without your Jesus. You feel that unless people convert to
your religion they are quite unhappy. Happiness is only what people make it to be,
not how some religion dictates. I used to be a Christian. I was a good Christian.
I went to Sunday school and everything. But emptiness is what I felt. Deep dark
emptiness. I could not even understand "Why?" I am now a Witch. I enjoy it very*

much. I am no longer sad or lonely. I have a clear purpose and I am free. Please write back.

Reply: I appreciate your letter, but I think you misunderstand what Christianity is about. You see, your words are all about how much happier you are now than you used to be. I take your former unhappiness seriously, and I'm sorry that you never got to the bottom of it. However, we Christians worship Christ because we believe He is the truth, not because He always makes us happy in this life. He desires final joy for each of His creatures, but it is certainly possible to delight in what is false and to sorrow in what is true; that is why false religions exist.

The other issue in your letter is condemnation. That's a red herring. If you really believed it wrong to condemn another person's religion, you wouldn't have written a letter in condemnation of mine. God is always to be praised; that which leads us away from God is always to be rejected; and the human beings whom God has made are always to be loved, as I, in His name, love you.

Peace be with you,
Professor Theophilus

WHAT IF?

Dear Professor Theophilus:

I've been thinking about "Not Much Use for God." What if Rachel gets rid of her anger, gets right with God, becomes the "messenger" to her brothers and all that jazz—yet her brothers don't listen anyway? What if their refusal to listen stirs her right back to her original position—being angry with God for not showing Himself to her? Besides the fact that she might be God's only messenger to her brothers, what other reason does she have for getting rid of her anger toward Him?

Let me put it another way. Assume the best, that Rachel's father died in Christ and will be raised with the rest of the dead in Christ at the last trump (or however that goes). I can see why this would comfort a believer whose beloved dead were also believers. But what if Rachel's brothers continued to spurn Christ until their death? Then what comfort would there be for her?

Reply: Of course you're right that Rachel's brothers might not respond, just as Rachel herself might not respond. The point isn't that helping her brothers is the only good reason to be reconciled with God. It's that she is irrational to blame God for the free decisions of human beings—whether her brothers' or her own. If she genuinely laid aside her anger and opened the doors of her sullen heart to the grace of God, she would soon discover many other reasons to trust Him. No one's motives for surrendering to Christ are pure; how amazing it is that He is willing to accept us on those terms. "I believe! Help my unbelief!"[24]

Peace be with you,
Professor Theophilus

GIVE ME ONE GOOD REASON

Dear Professor Theophilus:

My question is simple: Where do you derive your belief that the Christian faith has any power? I've read the Bible for years, but I simply see no power present in Christians that I don't see among non-Christians. For example, it seems that Christian males can't stop using pornography and masturbating to save their lives; you'd think it was a prerequisite for faith. It's amazing to me that they say, "Our God is an awesome God" while they can wallow in an addiction that God doesn't help.

That was my own situation, and a big reason for my letting go of Christianity. Thankfully, now that I am out of it, I experience far less desire (almost none, actually) for any of these activities. My true desire is for intimacy, just as a Christian's "should" be.

Furthermore, Christianity laid upon me a huge weight of guilt. I couldn't continue to sin, with full knowledge that I was sinning, and yet ask forgiveness. If I am going to sin (which happens every day), I might as well remove the guilt.

Now that I'm in the driver's seat, yes, I fail miserably every day, but there is no Christ sitting there telling the parable of the foolish virgins or the wasted talents; no Christ saying, "I do not come to condemn the world" while simultaneously condemning those who should know better and yet do not act upon their knowledge.

I am by no means a good man; I'm really quite a jerk whose alcohol intake is (consciously) increasing weekly. However, I see no power in the Scriptures, no power in Christianity, and no power in anything having to do with Christian faith that isn't readily available to me by other means. In fact, I'm beginning to think that I see less.

Thank you for your time, consideration, and help. My Christmas list last year had Wisdom, Judgment, Knowledge, and Understanding on it, and I hope you will help impart a little bit of each to me.

Reply: Thanks for your letter. You say your question is why I believe that Christian faith has power to deliver someone from bondage to sin and guilt. I wouldn't put it quite that way. Christ is the one with the power to deliver us, and faith is merely the door through which He comes to us. What faith means is trusting Him with our whole heart and mind and will, saying "Yes" to Him with everything that is in us. It isn't faith that delivers, but Christ who delivers; therefore we need faith in Christ.

The reason I believe that He has this power is that innumerable witnesses have testified to it. First are the witnesses in Scripture and Christian tradition. Far less in authority, but closer to me, are the witnesses among people whom I know. Last and least, I guess, is me. I too once abandoned Him, and if you had known me before I returned to Him, you wouldn't have believed that He could deliver me either.

Yet I don't think that why I believe these things is your real question. Let me tell you how I read your letter.

1. You say that before abandoning Christ, you had already sunk into compulsive masturbation, use of pornography, and abuse of alcohol.

2. You say that since abandoning Christ you are "in the driver's seat" and now experience "far less desire" for any of these things. However, these statements are contradicted by your later confession that your alcohol intake is actually increasing week by week. Plainly you are in trouble, and you are not in the driver's seat at all.

3. The statements are also contradicted by the reason you give for abandoning Christ—*if you were going to go on sinning*, you say, then you might as well not feel guilty about it. The intention, then, was to go on sinning. If that was your intention, why complain to Him that you carried it out?

4. Moreover, you *haven't* really escaped from the sense of guilt. Your letter is full of self-justifications, some of them quite absurd. I'm thinking, for example, of your claim that every Christian male is in bondage to pornography and masturbation. Nobody works *that* hard to justify himself unless he knows he needs to.

5. The reason that abandoning Christ didn't release you from the sense of guilt is that Christ wasn't your accuser in the first place; your conscience was. The burden you escaped when you abandoned Christ was His offer of forgiveness, and the reason it was a burden was that you refused to repent and accept it.

6. The further you run from the Source of help, the more you need

to deny that He can help you. The further your life spins out of control, the more you need to believe that you are in the driver's seat, adequate to save yourself.

And so when you ask me why I believe that Christ has the power to deliver a man like you from bondage, I read in your words an arrogant challenge combined with a desperate plea. The challenge is "Christ didn't help me before. Give me one good reason to believe that He can help me now!" The plea is "With my back to Christ, I can't see Him anymore. Please tell me, is He really there?"

As to the plea: Yes, He's really there, but you can't see Him unless you turn around. You need to be authentically sorry, which is different from just feeling guilty. You need to abandon your claim to self-ownership and control and turn yourself over to Him. Finally you need to reverse course, fleeing *from* your sin instead of into it. If you don't yet want to turn around, then at least begin wanting to want to. Implore Christ with all your heart to make you want to. Ask Him to have His way with you at last. Be patient; pray persistently. You have been hardening your heart for a long time, and it may take Him time to soften it.

As to the challenge: I can well believe that Christ didn't help you before, because whatever you may have told yourself at the time, the fact is that you didn't yet want His help. Make no mistake, being healed is a laborious process. You may fall, repent, and be picked up, fall, repent, and be picked up, many times before you begin to feel His strength flowing into your legs. On the way, there may be pain, and there may be humiliating discoveries. But you have to begin.

I foresee that one of the most difficult things for you may be returning to Christian fellowship. Just as you don't want to acknowledge your dependence on Christ, you may find it hard to confess your need of help to other Christians. But the Church is the Ark in which

Christ pilots us over the flood. You can either enter in or drown.

When you asked on your Christmas list for a little bit of Wisdom, Judgment, Knowledge, and Understanding, you were asking *Someone;* who else was it, but Him? If you accept such little bits as He sends, then He will send more.

Postscript: After receiving my reply, you wrote back, "I agree that my own heart convicted me, but I didn't see in Christ an offer of forgiveness. I grant that this has a huge chance of being faulty, and I will conduct research to test my claim."

If you didn't see in Christ an offer of forgiveness, try these! "Come unto me, all ye that travail and are heavy laden, and I will refresh you."[25] "God so loved the world, that he gave his only-begotten Son, to the end that all that believe in him should not perish, but have everlasting life."[26] "This is a true saying, and worthy of all men to be received, that Christ Jesus came into the world to save sinners."[27] "If any man sin, we have an Advocate with the Father, Jesus Christ the Righteous; and he is the perfect offering for our sins, and not for ours only, but for the sins of the whole world."[28]

I liked the ending to your second letter. You explained that it was your parents whom you had asked for Wisdom, Judgment, Knowledge, and Understanding. "They are Christians," you said, "so I'm sure that the Lord has been asked. I have not said in my heart, 'There is no God,' so there is still hope."

Yes, there is. My advice to you is to act on it.

Peace be with you,
Professor Theophilus

IT FEELS ALL FAKE

Dear Professor Theophilus:

I became a Christian when I was nine, but my parents got divorced shortly afterward, and I started having a lot of problems with my dad. These events caused me to drift away from God. I haven't seen my dad since I was 12, and over the years the pain from that has begun to heal. Since I've been in college, I've been trying to return to my faith — praying regularly, reading Scriptures, becoming active in church, being in community with other Christians, but I have to admit that it feels all fake. Every prayer I pray and every song I sing feels like I'm pretending to be someone else. I do believe in Christ and God's Word, but I can't feel God's presence in my life.

The one person I've shared this feeling with suggested to me that I couldn't see God as a loving father because my own father had been such a bad example. I have a feeling there is some truth to that, but I don't know how to fix it. I've spent a lot of time praying about this and thinking about the situation, without much luck. I'm basically at my rope's end and I'm worried that if I don't find some way to have a more intimate relationship with God, I won't be able to continue on this path.

Reply: I think you've hit the nail on the head. When people tell me about intellectual difficulties — lines of reasoning that make believing in God seem unreasonable — then I talk theology with them. What you've told me about, though, is something different. It isn't an intellectual difficulty, but a spiritual emptiness. There is a hole in your heart where God ought to be. If you hadn't already mentioned another hole in your life where your earthly father ought to be, I would have had to ask about that. God intended our earthly fathers to give us our first warm image of His heavenly Fatherhood; trusting Dad's gentleness, love, and strength should be like a first lesson in trusting God. If Dad lets you down, something down inside you feels like God will do that too. I know, it *seems* that you're calling but God isn't answering. Actually He's right there in the room. He's calling *you*, but you're holding Him at arm's length to keep from being hurt again.

Can you talk yourself into trusting Him? No, because trust is an aspect of faith, and faith is a gift of grace. On the other hand, He is offering the gift to you already. For now, your job is just to open your hands to receive it. Little by little is okay. Try to relax those clenched, white-knuckled fingers. Their muscles have been cramped a long time, so ask Him to uncramp them. You don't have to pretend that it isn't difficult. He knows. Be patient with Him, as He is patient with you.

Of course, opening clenched hands is a metaphor, a word-picture, so by now you must be asking what you can actually *do!* Since the puncture wound in your heart probably comes from your own broken family, I suggest that you begin by meditating on the Holy Family. Here's what I mean. Open your Bible and find Matthew 1:18–2:23 and Luke 1:1–2:52. Bookmark them. Start with the Matthew passage. It's not long, but don't read it all at once. Starting at the beginning, each day read a few verses of it—say, three to seven. Then think about these verses for just five minutes, focusing on the personalities and home life of Jesus, Mary, Joseph, and their relatives. That may not seem like much, but take it easy; if you're new to this sort of thing, five minutes may seem a long time. Stay focused, and read carefully, slowly, prayerfully, as though you were handling fine silks. Don't worry about what you're learning or not learning, feeling or not feeling; let Christ take care of that. Just think quietly. Don't quit. When you finish the Matthew passage—that may take many days—begin on the Luke passage. When you finish that one write again to tell me how you're doing.

As you practice this daily routine, you may think to yourself "I don't know what's supposed to be happening." Don't worry; you don't have to. *He* knows what you're supposed to be doing, and He'll help you. Be still, and take that same stillness into your worship with others at your church. One more thing: Remember that trusting our Father and obeying Him go together; you can't have one without the other.

Peace be with you,
Professor Theophilus

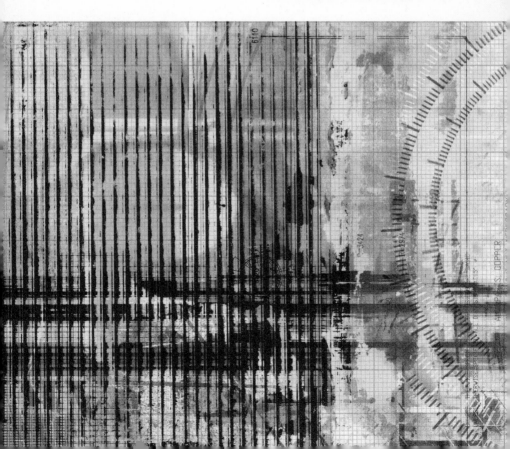

FLEEING TOWARD
GOD STUFF

CHAPTER EIGHTEEN

WHAT THIS SECTION IS ABOUT

The opening remarks for the previous section began with a short quotation from St. Augustine. That was to soften you up for this long one. Theophilus would approve; in fact it was his idea.

"The Maker of man became man that He, Ruler of the stars, might be nourished at the breast; that He, the Bread, might be hungry; that He, the Fountain, might thirst; that He, the Light, might sleep; that He, the Way, might be wearied by the journey; that He, the Truth, might be accused by false witnesses; that He, the Judge of the living and the dead, might be brought to trial by a mortal judge; that He, Justice, might be condemned by the unjust; that He, Discipline, might be scourged with whips; that He, the Foundation, might be suspended upon a cross; that Courage might be weakened; that Security might be wounded; that Life might die.

"To endure these and similar indignities for us, to free us, unworthy creatures, He who existed as the Son of God before all ages, without a beginning, consented to become the Son of Man in these recent years. He did this although He who submitted to such great evils for our sake had done no evil and although we, who were the recipients of so much good at His hands, had done nothing to merit these benefits."[29]

Any questions?

CHAPTER NINETEEN

NOT ENOUGH

ON LONGING FOR EVERYTHING TO BE MORE THAN IT IS

When I heard the two-fisted, alternating knock at my office door—*bappa-dappa-dap*—I called out, "Is that you, Peter?"

He entered and sat down. "How'd you know? Your back was to the hallway."

"I can't answer that question. It's against union rules."

"No, c'mon," he pleaded, "tell me."

I laughed. "The first clue is that double knock of yours; it's like a signature."

"What do you mean, *first* clue? Is there another?"

"Yes. This is No Class Week, the week before final exams."

"Sure, but what's that got to do with it?"

"Except for you, Peter, nobody drops in during No Class Week. Everyone is busy studying, or pretending to. But you do. That's been your pattern ever since that time four semesters ago—remember?—when you were depressed about going home for Christmas. It was the same time of year."

"I guess you're right."

Ruefully, I shook my head. "I shouldn't be giving away these professional secrets."

"Don't worry, I won't tell."

"So what *does* bring you here?"

"Oh, nothing."

"Out with it."

"Really. Nothing." He gave a heavy sigh.

"Listen to you," I laughed. "That doesn't sound like 'Really. Nothing.' It sounds more like 'Woe is me.'"

"No, really, I'm fine," he repeated. "In fact I think I'm making progress."

"What kind of progress?"

"Spiritual progress. I'm getting more mature as a Christian." He sighed again, as heavily as before.

I lifted an eyebrow. "I see how joyful you are about it."

"Sorry. It must be a high-ozone day or something."

"Or something. Do you want to tell me about this new maturity?"

"The main thing is that I'm scaling back my expectations," he replied.

"What do you mean?"

"I was always *wanting*. Do you follow me?"

"No. Do you mean that you were always wanting more 'stuff,' more material things?"

"More stuff, no. More something, yes. No, not more something; I was always yearning for things to be *something more*. I can't explain. They just weren't enough."

"Things like what?"

"Everything. Myself, my family, my friendships, my studies, my girlfriend, my church, even my senior project."

"Do you mean that you wanted everyone to be perfect?"

"Not that. We're supposed to practice mercy, right? Charity, lovingkindness, all that good stuff? So it couldn't be right for me to look down on others harshly. *I'm* far from perfect, and people put up with *me*."

"What did you want, then?"

"I guess I wanted all these things to *satisfy*. And they never did. I was asking more from things than they can give. That was immature."

He paused. I said nothing. In a few moments he continued. "Actually, I think that was my problem a few years ago—when I was so depressed about my family's Christmas."

"How so?"

"I told you that day that the problem was that Christ wasn't in it."

"I remember."

"Well, that was true enough. He wasn't, much. By the way, that's better now. But there was another problem, and that one hasn't changed. See, the problem wasn't just Christmas. The reason I'd wanted Christmas to be more than it can be was that I wanted *everything* to be more than it can be."

"And now?"

"I'm getting more mature. I've scaled back my expectations, like I said. I'm not expecting more from things than they can give anymore. Not Christmas, not family, not friendships, not even myself—nothing."

Again I was silent.

He said, "Just now I sighed again, didn't I?"

"Sure sounded like it," I said.

There was another pause. "I think that's because I'm not there yet," he said.

"Not where yet?"

"If only I could expect *nothing*, I'd know that I'd got there. If only I could let everything be only what it is. Then I wouldn't have any more of these immature disappointments." He looked out the window. "Maybe there would even be a kind of satisfaction in not expecting to be satisfied."

"Would there be?"

"I don't know. But I'm tired of being such a baby Christian."

"Why do you call this despondency 'Christian'?"

"Isn't that what it is?"

"It sounds more like Buddhism."

"I've never even studied Buddhism. Why do you say that?"

"Buddhists think suffering comes from desire. Their 'eightfold way' mentions 'right desire,' but their ultimate goal is to have no desire at all—no longing, no yearning, no aspiration. When that happens, they believe, they will no longer suffer disappointment, because they *won't be*. The illusion of individual existence will have been annihilated."

"I don't know about that annihilation stuff. But the killing of desire—isn't that biblical?"

"What makes you think so?"

"It's in the Bible. The other day I was reading it in Ecclesiastes. 'All things are full of weariness; a man cannot utter it.'"[30]

"Peter, Ecclesiastes was written before Christ. The author is baffled by the mysteries of death and futility. In his generation God hasn't yet fully revealed the basis of Christian hope."

"Then why is it in the Bible?"

"Because if you aren't acquainted with the hope that Christ brought—if you know nothing about the lifting of fallen things, the binding of broken things, the resurrection of the dead—then the view that it expresses is reasonable. For us who come after Him, everything is different, everything is changed. Paul says that what was written in former days was written so that we might have *hope*, not despair."[31]

"But if Christian hope hasn't been fulfilled yet, then for all practical purposes it makes no difference, right? I'm happy that Christ came and all that. But it's still true that nothing fully satisfies."

"In the Christian view, the task isn't to scale back our expectations. It's to ratchet them up even higher."

"You've got to be kidding."

"I've never been more serious."

"But if nothing fully satisfies—"

"Nothing but Christ Himself."

"Ye-es—"

"That thought shouldn't kill our yearning. It should make us yearn even more."

"For Him, you mean."

"Yes, for Him. Paul says that the creation waits with eager longing for the revealing of the sons of God—for us, redeemed in Him. The author of Ecclesiastes—whoever he was—could only see that everything is subjected to futility. Paul goes further. He says everything is subjected to futility *in hope*."[32]

"Is that where he talks about creation groaning like a woman in labor?"

"Yes, groaning for the sake of what is coming.[33] A bit like the way you've been groaning with those heavy sighs. By the way, Paul has something to say about your sighing, too."

"I suppose he says I shouldn't do it."

"Just the opposite. He'd say that you need to sigh *more*."

"More than I do already?"

"You didn't let me finish. I was going to add, 'But not in the same way.'"

"There's a wrong way?"

"Sure. You've been sighing in something close to hopelessness. Paul wants you to sigh in hope. According to him, we don't even know our hearts well enough to pray the right way. But the Holy Spirit knows them, and He helps out our prayers by adding His own sighs, too deep for words."[34]

"But if nothing satisfies except Him—like we've been saying—then all those other things I was talking about—friends, family, girlfriend, church, studies—"

"What about them?"

"Doesn't that make them worthless?"

"Why?"

"Just because they *aren't* God."

"Not at all. Didn't He create them? They reflect Him, don't they? In fact, aren't we His image?"

"Well—yes, I suppose."

"Then accept them as glimpses! Rejoice in them for that!"

"But they only sharpen that craving I've been trying to scale back. They just make me want *more*."

"Peter, that's just what they were meant to do to you. Don't long for more *from them*—but by all means long for more! Let every created mirror of God's uncreated glory sharpen your craving for God Himself, in person."

"Prof, you're killing me, talking this way. All those weird longings I was trying to stifle—they're coming up again inside me."

"They should come up again, Peter. Besides, it's Advent. Isn't that what the season is for?"

"What has Advent got to do with it? Isn't that just the season before Christmas? When we begin to celebrate?"

I laughed. "That's what department stores think. No, *Christmas* is the season of celebration. *Advent* is the season of yearning and anticipation."

"But how can we—if He already came—"

"He came, and He will come again."

"We're yearning for *two* things?"

"We reenact the yearning of Mary and Joseph for Jesus, and the yearning of all the Hebrew people who were waiting for Messiah. Just like a spiritual time machine. At the same time, we sharpen our yearning for His return."

"How do we do *that*?"

"Peter, Peter, you know the answer to that question, don't you?"

Peter hesitated. Then he nodded. "We do it the way they did."

"How is that?"

"Total surrender."

I smiled. A student group was caroling on the quad. The strains of an Advent hymn came faintly through the window:

Zion hears the watchmen singing,
And all her heart with joy is springing,
She wakes, she rises from her gloom . . .

"You see," I said to him, "you were right to want something more."

THE COMEBACK SIN, PART 1

SOME SINS JUST KEEP COMING BACK

My hands paused at the keyboard. Was that someone at my door?

I peered out into the hallway. Nobody there. Back to typing. *Tappety-tap.*

The same noise came again. A sort of shuffle, like a shoe against the floor. Probably just the air conditioning system, but it was distracting. I got up to close the door—

And almost collided with a human body. "Jordan! What are you doing out here? Are you stalking me?"

"No! I—gosh. No, no. Sorry. I—gosh. Sorry. I—"

"Relax, Jordan, I'm joking." I eyed him. "You're *lurking*, though, aren't you? Why don't you just come in?"

Sheepishly, he accepted the invitation. "I was trying to get up the nerve."

"Am I so formidable? You've never been afraid of me before."

"It isn't *you*. It's what I want you to do."

"Do you need a letter of recommendation or something?"

"No. I want you to pray for me." He turned pink.

"Me?"

He nodded. "That is, if you don't mind."

"Certainly, but—"

"I'm sorry, I'm sorry, I know it's a lot of trouble. I probably shouldn't even—"

I smiled. "Jordan, it's no trouble at all. I was only going to say,

'Certainly, but about what?'"

"About—what?"

I nodded. "First word, 'about,' preposition. Second word, 'what,' inter-rogative pronoun. What would you like me to pray for you about?"

"I'm not sure that I want to tell you."

"Then don't. I'll pray a very general prayer, just asking God to bless you. Will that do?"

He hesitated. "I need a very specific kind of help."

"God knows what you need, Jordan."

"That's true. Still. I wish you could—well—maybe I should tell you anyway. Will this be confidential?"

"Of course." I swept my hand toward the wall. "No listening devices. No sound recorders. No bugs. Now what is this about?"

"I want you to pray for me for deliverance."

"Deliverance?"

"Yes. I've got a problem with a—I don't know what to call it—a comeback sin."

"What do you mean by a 'comeback' sin? Do you mean an old sin you thought you had conquered, that has come back to trouble you again?"

"No, it's a new one. For me. But it does keep coming back. I'm talking about the kind of sin where—well—you do it, you repent, you do it again, you repent again—in tears, even—but you do it again anyway. Where you can't seem to get off the treadmill."

"That used to be called a 'besetting' sin."

"You understand, then?"

"I think so. St. Paul even talks about besetting sin. 'I do not under-stand my own actions. For I do not do what I want, but I do the very thing I hate.'"

"Yeah—Romans 7. I've been reading it over and over. A morose passage, that one."

"I wouldn't say that. It begins morosely, but it ends on a note of joy."

"He says, 'Wretched man that I am! Who will deliver me from this body of death?' You call that joyful?"

"But he answers his own question, doesn't he? 'Thanks be to God through Jesus Christ our Lord!'"

"I believe that, Professor Theophilus. Really I do. But at the moment, I'm not experiencing it."

I was silent for a moment. "Paul doesn't say that deliverance will be easy or quick."

"No. That's why I asked you to pray for me. For the Holy Spirit to deliver me from my—um—besetting sin."

"I will. Count on it."

"Thanks."

Jordan didn't leave.

"Is there anything else I can do?"

He hesitated. "Yes."

"Name it."

"I know I'm not giving you much to go on, but—do you have any advice?"

I considered. "Maybe. It would have to be very general advice."

"You mean because you don't know what my besetting sin is?"

"Right. And because there are a lot of other things I don't know about you. And a lot of things about God that I don't yet understand."

"Anything would help."

"For what it's worth, then. First, Jordan, you're not alone in this. A lot of people go through what you're going through."

"You're saying that this is common?"

"Sure. For one person, resentment may be a besetting sin. It gnaws at him. He forgives and forgives, but his heart keeps returning to its bitterness. For another person, vanity may be a besetting sin.

Try as he may to think about other things, his thoughts keep coming back to what other people are thinking about him. Or the problem may have to do with envy, with sex, with hot temper, with spiritual pride—wherever your weakness is, that's where the Adversary will goad you."

"That sounds obvious now that you say it, but I hadn't thought about it."

"Did you think you were the only person who struggles?"

"I guess I did. But Prof, why is this *happening?* I could understand if I was like I was before."

"What do you mean, 'like I was before'?"

"I used to be not very serious about my faith."

I smiled. "I remember when you changed."

"Yeah. Well, that's over. Now it's just the opposite. I stopped holding back. There's nothing I want more than God. I can't stand it when I disappoint Him. But I'm betraying Him *every day.*"

"Do you think that only people who *aren't* trying to follow Christ should suffer besetting sins?"

"Wouldn't that make more sense? Like this. Say some guy goes in heavy for a certain kind of sin. He never gives a thought to seeking God. Then he changes. He yields to Christ. He becomes a Christian, or maybe, if he was an unserious Christian before, he becomes a serious one. Okay, those old habits will probably weigh him down, right? Getting free of a load like that might take a lot of time, a lot of sweat, and a lot of grace. Right?"

"Right."

"But I've been pretty serious about my faith for quite a while now. And I never went through that."

"No?"

"I've sinned sometimes, sure. I've had things to repent, sure. I've had struggles—lots of them—little struggles. But it's not until *now* that

I've been in *this* kind of battle. I'm trying to follow God *more*—but it's like I'm getting *worse*. How can that even *happen?* It seems impossible."

"Why does it seem impossible?"

"It's obvious. Let me show you." Jordan rummaged in his backpack for paper and pencil. He drew a broad, flattish triangle resting on its base with the point sticking upward. "I'm a mountain climber, right? I'm making a spiritual ascent. My artwork isn't good, but this is the mountain."

I smiled. "If you say so."

"No, really. Now look." He made a black scribble at the bottom of the picture. "These are the rocks and boulders and thornbushes at the *base* of the mountain—vices and bad habits and sins. They make it hard to get started. Big struggle. Get what I mean?"

"Sure."

"But look here," he said. He put the tip of the pencil on the side of the triangle, above the scribble. "Once you're past the rocks and all that other junk, the slope is smooth and the going should be steady."

He threw down the pencil, threw himself back in his chair, and folded his arms across his chest. "But the going *isn't* smooth. I don't get it. It doesn't make sense."

I laughed. "Jordan, you haven't proven that the higher you go, the smoother the slope becomes. You've only assumed that. What if the mountain is more like this?" I drew another triangle. "That's the mountain." Instead of making a scribble at the bottom of the picture, like he did, I made one halfway up. "But on this mountain, you don't meet the worst rocks and things until you've been climbing a while. See?"

He nodded.

"Or like this," I continued. I drew a shape like the Eiffel Tower —broad at the bottom, narrow and sharp at the top. "No rocks, no thorns, but the higher you climb, the steeper the slope."

He nodded again.

"Or even like this," I said. I drew another triangle, but this time I erased part of one side and redrew it in a zigzag. Instead of going up, up, up to the apex, the new line went up, down, then up again. "This mountain is the trickiest of all. Halfway up the slope, there's a crevasse. An unwary soul may climb a thousand feet, take a false step, and fall all the way to the bottom."

I glanced over to Jordan. This time he didn't nod. He looked at me aghast. "If it's like *that*," he said, "how can you *smile* about it? And what can you *do?*"

THE COMEBACK SIN, PART 2

WHY DOESN'T HOLINESS COME FASTER?

Jordan had been talking to me about a besetting sin. I had just given him the unwelcome news that his assumptions about sin and spiritual progress were incorrect. There never comes a point in this life where struggles disappear.

"If it's like *that*," he was saying, "how can you smile about it? And what can you do?"

I laughed. "Which do you want to know first? How I can smile about it, or what you can do?"

"How you can smile," he grumped.

"For two reasons. The first is that Christ is right there with us. He takes the worst burdens on Himself. What else did you think He was doing on the Cross?"

"I thought that was long ago," he said.

"Long ago in time," I replied, "but in eternity, it's always right now. God doesn't *change*, Jordan. Everything that He has ever done, in a certain sense He is always doing. He is carrying your burdens right now."

"What's the other reason?"

"That if we cooperate with the gift of His grace, we will, slowly, make progress. Not at the rate that we wish, not with the ease that we wish, not without tears. But we do make progress—and there is joy on the slope too. Christ Himself is the rope by which the Father helps pull us up, if only we hang on and cooperate."

Jordan was still displeased. "I don't see why we *shouldn't* be able to climb at the rate that we wish. Why doesn't He give *more* grace? Doesn't He *want* us to make better progress up the mountain?"

"I think He always takes us by the swiftest route He can."

"Not in my case."

I studied him. "How do you know that?"

"What do you mean, how do I know? God doesn't want me to sin, right?"

"Right."

"He promises help, right?"

"Right."

"He knows that I'm having a problem, right?"

"Right."

"So if He really wanted to take me up the slope by the swiftest route He could, He'd remove the temptation."

"Has it occurred to you," I asked, "that allowing you to experience the temptation might be a part of His grace?"

"How could *that* be?"

"Perhaps the very thing you needed to learn most of all at this point in your life was what He said to Paul—'My grace is sufficient for you, for my power is made perfect in weakness.'"[35]

"But I already know that His grace is sufficient for me."

"Do you? Haven't you just been telling me that it's *not?* Haven't you been arguing in the clearest possible terms that He *hasn't* been giving you enough grace?"

"But that's because I'm struggling!"

"That statement only shows that you feel *justified* in saying that His grace is insufficient. It hardly shows that you think it *is* sufficient."

He made no reply, but his color grew somewhat heightened.

I continued. "And think of how you were speaking a few minutes ago, when you were explaining how much easier things used to be."

"What did I say?"

"That you'd sinned *sometimes*. That you'd had *little* struggles. How does that sound to you?"

"It sounds accurate."

"How would it sound to you if someone else had said it?"

He hesitated. "I'd say it sounded smug."

"So is it possible that the greatest grace God could have given you at this point—the greatest help that He could have given you in getting up the mountain—might have been cutting your pride down to size?"

His color heightened further. "So you're saying that maybe I've been flattering myself. Taking credit for what really came from Him."

"I'm only asking, Jordan. I don't know. There are lots of different reasons why a person might begin to have greater trouble with temptation than he used to have. The cause might be something much simpler than pride—like not getting enough sleep, so that your defenses are weakened. But if you ask me whether you *may* have been just a little smug, then I think you should consider the possibility."

Embarrassed, he changed the subject. "What about my other question?"

"What other question?"

"I asked what I can *do* about my comeback sin. Prof, are you smiling *again*?"

"Perish the thought. But haven't we already been talking about what to do about your comeback sin?"

"I don't see how."

"What was it that we were saying might be the very thing you need to learn most of all at this point in your life?"

"Um—what Paul had to learn. 'My grace is sufficient for you, for my power is made perfect in weakness.'"

"If so, then the first thing you have to do is learn it. I don't think you can expect to make further progress until you do."

Jordan shifted in his seat. "What if my problem *isn't* that? What if you've misdiagnosed it?"

"I may have," I conceded. "After all, I'm not all-wise, and even after this conversation there are a lot of things about you that I don't know. I don't even know what kind of sin your besetting sin is. So I could be wildly off."

I looked him in the eye. "But if you're thinking of getting yourself off the hook, forget it. Whether the details of my diagnosis are right or wrong, at the bottom of every sin problem there is always *some* spiritual problem. It might be taking credit for God's grace — it might be anger toward Him — it might be incomplete repentance — it might be something else. But if you're serious about dealing with the sin problem, you have to start dealing with the spiritual problem."

There was a long pause.

At last he said, "What else can I do?"

"The rest is all practical."

"What do you mean?"

"There are certain practical steps anyone can take to make a temptation less troublesome. What they are depend on what your temptation is. I'm not asking you to tell me. But any sin can become a besetting sin. For Felix it may be drunkenness. For Sheila it may be resentment. For Edgar it may be sexual immorality."

"Felix I get. His practical steps would be pouring his liquor down the drain and joining a twelve-step group. Start with Sheila. What would her practical steps be? Avoiding the people who irritate her?"

"Maybe. But suppose that her bitterness is easily provoked, even toward her friends, and even for little things that shouldn't upset her. She couldn't very well avoid everyone, could she? And she shouldn't try."

"I guess not."

"But she could *pray* for the people toward whom she's bitter."

"How is that 'practical'?"

"It's amazingly difficult to be bitter toward someone whom you're praying for."

"Praying how? Like 'God, please forgive that rat Marsha'?"

I laughed. "What if Marsha hasn't been a rat? But even if she has been, why not this? It's better anyway. Sheila could pray, 'God, I know I've been bitter toward Marsha. Please help her to get over the flu.' And she could follow up by taking Marsha some hot chicken soup."

His face bland, Jordan asked, "What about your other example?"

"What about it?"

"I can't see any 'practical steps' that a person could take if the sin that kept coming back was sexual impurity."

"Why not?"

"Because that kind of problem is inside. There are—certain urges."

"The problem isn't *just* inside," I answered. "Suppose Edgar keeps going too far with Darla. Anything that makes it hard to stop is already too far. Obviously, then, he shouldn't do anything with Darla that gets his motor running."

"What if just holding hands with her gets his motor running?"

"Then he shouldn't hold hands with her. But do you really know anyone for whom just holding hands is that overpowering?" I saw from his face that he didn't.

"Second, he can stop doing all the *other* things that get his motor running. Watching certain television programs, reading certain magazines, even hanging out in certain places."

"He might say that's his recreation."

"Then he needs to stop thinking of sexual arousal as a form of recreation, doesn't he?"

He looked startled. "I guess he does."

"Third, he can stop spending time with Darla *alone*. They won't be so tempted if they spend all their time with their friends, or at least in places where other people are around."

He grinned. "Darla might not think much of that idea."

"The fourth practical thing he can do is choose a girlfriend who does." I paused. "Jordan, is any of this helpful to you?"

"Prof, I'm not saying that any of those is *my* sin."

"That's not what I'm asking."

"Well—yes. It's helpful." He hesitated. "But I'm still asking you to pray for me."

I smiled. "That's the fifth practical thing."

CHAPTER TWENTY-TWO

WHO'S CALLING?

IS THERE A WAY TO FIND OUT THE WILL OF GOD?

"Hello?" I intoned. "Who's calling? . . . I said, who's calling? . . . *Which* Bill? I know three . . . Oh, *Jill*, how are you? . . . What do you mean, who am I? Didn't you just call *me*? . . . I'm sorry, I thought you were a different Jill. This is Theophilus . . . I said *Theophilus* . . . M. E. Theophilus . . . No, there is no Theodoropoulos here . . . No, that is not my first name. You must have dialed the . . . Yes, I am *quite* sure I am not Milton Theodoropoulos. I hope you find him. Good-bye."

A sound of suppressed laughter came from the door. I swung around to see Mark. "Sorry," he said, "I couldn't help overhearing." His grin widened. "It was pretty funny, though. 'Who's calling?' Sounds like you and I have the same problem."

I waved him to a seat. "What problem is that?"

"Calling. Vocation. I still don't know what God wants me to do with my life. A couple of times I thought He was calling, but it was just a wrong number."

"I see." I said with a smile. "What telephone are you using?"

"What do you mean?"

"How do you discern God's will?"

"Oh, bother. People have suggested all kinds of methods to me."

"Like what?"

"When I was in high school, my uncle told me that whenever he needed to know God's will, he opened the Bible at random, read the first verse that met his eyes, then did whatever it told him."

"So you tried it?"

"Don't laugh. At first it seemed to work. One time I asked God whether I should go out with this really pretty girl named Melissa. When I opened the Bible, the first verse that met my eye was Proverbs 6:25: 'Do not desire her beauty in your heart, and do not let her capture you with her eyelashes.' So I asked, 'Then who *should* I go out with?' This time when I opened the Bible, the first verse that met my eye was Isaiah 55:12: 'You shall go out with joy.' So I asked out Joy."

"You shouldn't have asked me not to laugh. What opened your eyes?"

"Two things. First, Joy said no."

"What was the other?"

"Well," said Mark, "one day I happened to ask that same uncle why he'd taken up cigarettes. He said, 'God wanted me to smoke.' I asked, 'How'd you know that?' He said, 'Well, I opened the Bible at random and saw 1 Corinthians 6:19: 'Do you not know that your body is a temple . . . ?' Then I opened it again and saw Revelation 15:8: 'The temple was filled with smoke.' So that settled it."

I hid my smile in my coffee cup.

"That's when I figured it out," Mark said. "We were taking passages out of context and filling them with meanings God never intended."

"Good lesson. What other methods have people suggested to you?"

"What *haven't* they suggested? The organist for my church's college choir is big on miraculous experiences, like when Moses saw the burning bush and when Paul was struck down by a vision on the road to Damascus."

"I don't doubt that God sends visions and performs miracles," I said, "but it doesn't seem His routine way of making His will known."

"That's what I think," he answered. "I told her that not many people see burning bushes or lights from heaven."

"How did she reply?"

"She said, 'Maybe they're not looking.' Then she told me the story about how she decided to go into the religious music field. Something about a missing cross pendant that turned up inside a piano. I'm sure she made the right decision, but I thought that was a pretty silly reason for making it. I figured she'd dropped it there. She was reading a private meaning into a coincidence."

"Like when you and your uncle read private meanings into the Bible."

"Exactly."

"You implied that you've rejected a *lot* of different methods for discerning the will of God," I answered, "but so far you've only mentioned two. Depending on how you count, maybe three."

"Yeah. The Random Finger Method, the Miraculous Event Method, and, um, let's say the Striking Coincidence Method."

"So what are all these many others?"

"A deacon at my church mentioned what you might call the Casting Lots Method. I know people tried to find God's will by casting lots in Old Testament times, but it worries me that the New Testament mentions it only once, in Acts 1, when the Church was just getting started. If the Church gave up casting lots, maybe there was a good reason."

"Go on."

"Aren't you going to give me any help here, Prof?"

"So far you don't need it. You're doing fine. What's next?"

"Well, a guy I know who's in seminary advised what he called the Putting Out a Fleece Method. When he needs to know God's will he prays, 'God, if You want me to do such-and-such, show me by doing so-and-so.'"

"Like Gideon did in Judges 6."

"Right. There was some fleece, and Gideon prayed—never mind, you know the story."

"But didn't Gideon's prayer show *lack* of faith, Mark? In the story, God had *already* made clear what Gideon was supposed to do."

"That's what the chaplain for my college group pointed out. So it doesn't seem like putting out a fleece is such a good idea after all—at least not until every other way of seeking God's will has failed."

"Go on."

"My roommate follows what he calls the Open Door Method. In 1 Corinthians 16, Paul mentions that he was going to stay in Ephesus until Pentecost because a wide 'door' for effective work had 'opened' to him. So according to the Open Door Method, whenever God opens a door for you, you should take advantage of it right away."

"And does that seem reasonable to you?"

"At first it did, but after thinking about it I've changed my mind."

"Why?"

"Because in 2 Corinthians 2, Paul mentions another door that opened to him in another town. He *didn't* take advantage of that one, because he couldn't find his partner Titus. So I think 'open door' must just mean an opportunity. Not every opportunity is a sign of what God wants you to do."

"I agree."

"My other roommate follows the *Closed* Door Method. When an obstacle arises to your plan, assume that God's will is behind the obstacle, and back off. But that makes even less sense. In 2 Corinthians 10, Paul doesn't say, 'We back off from proud obstacles to the knowledge of God'; he says, 'We destroy them.'"

"Cut to the chase. Where does all this leave you?"

"There's one method of finding God's will that I'm still considering."

"What way is that?"

"I guess you could call it the Still Small Voice Method. You know, like in 1 Kings 19, when Elijah is fleeing, desperate to know the will of God, and he hears the 'still small voice.' I love that story. I know it almost by heart."

"When the Lord passed by Elijah," I said, "a great and mighty wind tore the mountains in pieces, but the Lord was not in the wind."

Taking up the story, Mark continued. "After the wind came an earthquake, but the Lord was not in the earthquake."

"After the earthquake came a fire," I responded, "but the Lord was not in the fire."

Mark spoke the conclusion. "And after the fire, a still small voice."

We were silent for a few moments.

"But Mark," I asked, "how is that a *method*?"

He was surprised. "You listen for the still small voice. Once you've identified it, that's the voice of God."

"What do you take this still small voice to be? A literal voice?"

"No, it's a — well, an inward impression or something."

"And how do you identify it?"

"I suppose it would be like a feeling."

"But there are a lot of feelings, aren't there? At the times that you're most in need of God's guidance, don't you often have several at once? So if the still small voice is a feeling, which feeling is it?"

"The stillest, smallest one."

"Does that mean the weakest one?"

He seemed confused. "I guess so."

"Then is this what you mean by your Still Small Voice Method? First look inward to your feelings, then see which are strong and which are weak, and finally, whatever the weakest one prompts you to do, do that?"

Mark reddened a little. "When you put it that way — I guess not.

But if *that's* not the method for identifying the still small voice, what is?"

"I didn't say there was a method. You did."

"What do you mean?"

"The story doesn't teach a *method* for discerning the will of God; what it teaches is that the will of God has to be discerned. The reason God's voice in the story is called still and small is that sometimes — as in this case — it isn't easy to do that."

"I didn't say the still small voice would be *obvious*."

"For Elijah, the problem wasn't that it was less than obvious, but that it wasn't what he wanted to hear."

"What do you mean?"

"If God's will *wasn't* obvious to him, it should have been. He had no reason to flee. Yes, he'd been threatened by the king, but by the power of God, he had just won his greatest victory. So why was he running away? What was he doing out there in the wilderness, all alone?"

"That's just what the still small voice asked him."

"Yes, and it told him to go back."

"You're saying that there *isn't* any method?"

I hesitated. "Not what you've been calling a method. Discernment has its own spiritual laws, and of course they have to be followed. If you want to call that a method, you can, but it's not like what you've been calling methods. Those so-called methods are just gimmicks — not ways of discerning God's will, but ways of avoiding discernment."

"So what do I have to do? Become a prophet or a mystic or something?"

I smiled. "The first law of discernment is Preparation. Seek God's help to become the right kind of person inside — develop the right spiritual habits. Otherwise you haven't a chance to find His will."

"Habits like what?"

"The habit of prayer. The habit of faith. The habit of distrusting the desires and devices of your own devious heart. The habit of patience—what Scripture calls 'waiting on the Lord'—because God might guide you only a few steps at a time. The habit of submission in every matter where you *already* know His will, for He has already blessed us with revelation. The habit of seeking wisdom—learning to know His ways. Most of all, the habit of loving Him with your whole heart, and of loving your neighbor as yourself."

"Pardon me for saying so, Professor T, but that all sounds pretty obvious."

"It wasn't obvious to the people who invented the gimmicks. Or to you when you were following them."

"Hmm. I guess not. What's the second law?"

"The second law of discernment is Meditation. In the presence of God, contemplate all the relevant features of the decision. Seek human advice too—the Proverbs say, 'Without counsel plans go wrong, but with many advisers they succeed.'[36] Since you want to know how God is calling you, the relevant features of *your* decision include your gifts and talents, your weaknesses and tendencies to sin, the courses of action available, and the opportunities each one affords to glorify God and serve your neighbor. You come last, of course."

"But that all sounds pretty obvious too."

"Does it?"

"Yes. What's the third law?"

"The third and final law of discernment is Obedience. You follow whatever path is wisest."

Mark was silent for a few seconds. "That's all you're going to say?"

"That's all there is."

"But that's what I came here to find out," he pleaded. "How do I *know* which path is wisest?"

I looked at him with compassion. "If you have to ask the meaning of the third law," I said, "then you aren't taking the other two seriously."

He didn't understand yet, but I knew that in time he would.

RUNNING TOWARD GOD

LETTERS

PROVING IT

Dear Professor Theophilus:

Okay. I've gone to church, I've heard the gospels, and I think I believe that Christ died to save us from sin and all that, but I am a science-oriented person and unfortunately I usually need proof to believe in something. So how can I prove to myself that this stuff is true?

Reply: It depends on what you mean by "proof." If you are asking for an argument so compelling that it makes doubt impossible and eliminates the need for faith, there's no such thing. Logical reasoning doesn't eliminate the need to take anything on trust; in fact it presupposes taking certain things on trust. This is true in science too. You see, anything whatsoever can be doubted. You can doubt that there is any connection between your reasoning and the world. You can doubt that there is a world at all. You can doubt that two and two will always equal four. Hey, maybe you *dreamed* that experiment.

But if you are asking for good reasons to believe that Christ died to save us from sin and all that, then yes, there are good reasons. For a good example, take a look at the first part of C. S. Lewis's short book *Mere Christianity*.[37] Lewis begins with two basic pieces of data—the existence of a moral law that we did not make ourselves, and our inability to live up to it. First he considers the various ways to explain away the data, then he considers all of the ways to explain it. In the end, the Christian explanation is the only one that accounts for all the facts. Take a look at the argument and see what you think.

Peace be with you,
Professor Theophilus

STRUGGLING WITH HELL

Dear Professor Theophilus:

I have a problem. I know God exists. I know God is just. I know God is love. But why doesn't He make it a little more obvious just who He is? I have this answer: God must keep Himself partially hidden from us, because if we saw Him in all His glory, we would all perish (speaking of those not redeemed by Christ). Thus, it's because of His love that He hides Himself — He allows us time to repent. But still, that answer just doesn't seem to satisfy my heart. Surely He could hide Himself in a little more obvious way? At least just make us choose between His existence and His nonexistence, rather than the smorgasbord of actual religions?

Why does God allow so many religions to come into being? Each claims to be the one true way. But obviously, they can't all be. It's small comfort to be told "God is not willing that any should perish, but that all should come to repentance." Yes, it helps me to believe in the goodness and love of God, yet I know that millions and millions of souls will be lost forever in tormenting fires. The Bible clearly says that many will end up there. Maybe even most — broad is the path that leads to destruction, but narrow the way that leads to life.

I tell you right now that I am really struggling with the reality of hell. Am I supposed to look at the millions passing me by going to hell and "rejoice in the Lord always"? And I suppose I could always go with the answer "what does the clay have to say to the potter" or perhaps "What is that to thee? Follow thou

Me." Yet still I don't feel satisfied. How do you deal with it?

Reply: That's a long question. Actually it's a lot of questions, but the two main questions are these: Why doesn't God make His reality more obvious, and why does He allow millions and millions to go to hell? I'll answer by examining your assumptions. You assume (1) that the reality of God *isn't* obvious, (2) that people can't *help* being confused about Jesus, and (3) that millions and millions *do* go to hell. As to assumption (1), the implication of Romans 1 is that the reality of God *is* obvious. Paul doesn't scold the pagans because they ought to know about God and they don't, but because they do know about God and pretend to themselves that they don't. He says everyone *really* knows about the Creator; we just torture ourselves (or comfort ourselves) with the idea that we don't — and our reasons for doing so aren't pretty.[38] I know that's not the fashionable view, but I think it's the biblical view, and I think — as a former atheist — that it's true.

As to assumption (2), Jesus says plainly that His sheep know His voice and follow Him.[39] In other words, none of His sheep hear His voice and yet fail, at last, to recognize it. "Yes," you may ask, "but what about those to whom the Gospel has not come, or to whom it has been misrepresented?" Christ hasn't told us His provisions concerning them — but do you really want to tell the God whose very being is love that you won't trust Him to do the right thing unless He lets you in on the details so you can judge for yourself? Jesus also said, "And I have other sheep, that are not of this fold; I must bring them also, and they will heed my voice."[40] What that tells us is "I know all about your fears for them; trust Me."

Now as to assumption (3): The Bible doesn't tell us that millions and millions are going to hell. It doesn't give any figure at all. It says that the road is broad — meaning easy — but that doesn't tell us how many are on it. It says few are on the road to life, but even a large number may seem few to a God who is unwilling that any should perish.[41] There may or may not be millions and millions on that road; God simply hasn't told us. So there's no point torturing ourselves about that either. We know that He won't interfere if someone is determined to reject Him. But we also know His attitude toward suffering; He let Himself be nailed to the Cross, taking the worst of our suffering upon Himself.

Peace be with you,
Professor Theophilus

THE AUGUSTINIAN

Dear Professor Theophilus:

I'm currently a junior. For the last four years, I've been going back and forth between a pursuit of God and a pursuit of pleasure. The typical American ideal of Christianity is starting to wear thin, and I feel like nothing short of a drastic change in my relationship with God will rectify the situation. What must I do to have a permanent walk with God? More accurately, what must be done to make my walk with God a fruitful one?

Reply: That's a better question than I can answer briefly, but I'll try. You need to do several things, and I mean right away. There is no time to lose.

Make up your mind once and for all which one you are going to pursue with all your heart — God or pleasure — because God makes no guarantee that He will show the riches of His love to those who would rather have something else.

Realize that following Christ is more like joining the marines than like going to summer camp. It's about joy, yes, and greater than your pleasures, but it's also about sweat and toil.

Get back into *regular* Christian fellowship, not only on campus, but also with a real church.

Form friendships with mature Christians of the same sex who can show you the ropes.

Get rid of the empty idea that it's even *possible* to have enduring pleasure apart from the One who created it.

Stop blaming the Church — which, after all, is made up of sinners just like you — for your own inability to make up your mind.

Pray like crazy.

You remind me of St. Augustine before his conversion, who prayed to God, "Grant me chastity and continence, but not yet."[42] Some seekers need gentle encouragement. You need something more like a kick in the pants, don't you think? Now, really, don't you?

Peace be with you,
Professor Theophilus

AMBUSHED BY DOUBT

Dear Professor Theophilus:

Although I have considered myself a Christian for many years, for most of this time I was a "pseudo-Christian." I had only a fuzzy faith that I really didn't have to back up. During the past year or so this has changed. I can honestly say that I love Jesus and try to emulate Him in every way I can.

Then, just this week, I got news that my uncle is dying. He has literally drunk himself under. It's no real surprise to any of the family. Thinking it was time for him to turn himself around, I picked up a copy of a Christian book for him — and then it hit me. Doubt — after doubt — after doubt. Suddenly my own faith was assaulted in a large way. I've read a lot of apologetics and found most of it pretty good, but certain things are dogging me.

In a collection edited by Geisler and Hoffman, Why I Am a Christian, *I read your chapter titled "Why I Am Not an Atheist."*[43] *You talked about the long form of suicide, saying that in your atheist days, "There was no need to bother with the taking of poison or the slashing of wrists, because it was all going on in my mind. In one long, interminable prolongation of nightfall, the light went out and went out and went out, all without the inconvenience of physical death." I've got to tell you that right now, I feel like that. My family is looking at me funny and wondering why I'm acting so strange, but I really don't want to open this up to them. They couldn't help in this case, so I'm masking it as best I can.*

I truly desire Christ and need to know if what I'm reading weekly in the Bible is fact, not just embellishment or character building. Thanks so much.

Reply: Take heart: You are experiencing a relatively normal attack of doubt. It feels worse than it is because it's your first time and you didn't expect it. I think you will find, though, that it is your faith which is reasonable and rational, not the doubt.

What you are experiencing is something that many new or newly serious Christians experience. For some, doubt strikes immediately after conversion. For others, it strikes the moment they begin trying to lead a godly life. For still others, like you, it happens the first time they are called to go out on a limb—the first time they are called to do something which may make a difference to the life of someone else. Like your uncle.

There are two reasons why new Christians sometimes suffer this experience. One reason is the nervousness which is natural after big decisions. After all, there is no bigger decision than following Christ. Real estate agents call such nervousness "buyer's remorse" because a lot of home-buyers start worrying that the house is no good the moment they sign the mortgage papers. Newly engaged and newly married people sometimes feel panicky too. This passes. Trust me.

The second reason is that the Adversary hates your faith. There was no need to attack it before because it was so fuzzy. As soon as you began to take it seriously, he tried to blast it. But you're not helpless; this is an opportunity to exercise your faith muscles. Pray — and bear in mind that the mere fact that you can think of an objection to faith doesn't mean that you actually have good reason to abandon it! One can always think of objections; if I try, I can think of a dozen reasons why I *might* be hallucinating, or why my wife *might* be having an affair. But do I have good reason to abandon my trust in my senses, my memory, or my wife? No.

Of course you're right to seek out the answers to your specific questions. I responded to some of them in the private version of this letter. Keep seeking, but don't shut out the Church and the Christian members of your family from your distress. The Christian life is not a solitary life, and they may be far more help than you think, in ways you can't foresee. In the meantime, go on serving Christ. Visit your uncle. Talk with him. Love him. Take him the book. The very act of doing so will open the shutters in the shadowed room of doubt. Paralysis is the Adversary's ploy.

Finally, remember that faith is not the feeling of trust, but trust. You can go on living your faith even if from time to time the feelings seem to sputter. God will bless you for doing so, and someday *you* will be giving advice to someone who is struggling with doubt. After you've come through this attack, you'll be a battle veteran. Read what Paul says about spiritual warfare in Ephesians 6 and strap on the full armor of faith. Go with God, soldier.

Postscript: After receiving my reply, you wrote back, "Just thought you should get an update. My uncle made a comeback just long enough to talk to a minister and set himself right with Christ. A month before, I got over my doubt attack and sent him the book with a personal letter. Did my book and letter matter? I'm not sure, but I know they didn't hurt. Isn't it strange the way things work?"

Yes, it is: strange and wonderful.

Peace be with you,
Professor Theophilus

WHERE DO I BEGIN?

Dear Professor Theophilus:

I am a recent college graduate who suddenly finds herself feeling unfulfilled. I always clung to my schoolwork and had a ravenous appetite for literature. I earned two degrees and a minor, and I graduated with honors. I don't list these accomplishments to brag, but to demonstrate that getting what the world offers can leave a person as empty as before. While gorging my mind, I neglected my spirit.

A line in your online article about your conversion, "Escape From Nihilism," struck to the heart of what I've been feeling. You wrote that "given the meaninglessness of things," you had "no reason to do or not do anything at all. This is a terrible thing to believe."[44] I'm feeling that meaninglessness now, and it's terrible. I can't find meaning in anything anymore, big or small. I'm searching for God, but I'm afraid — of what I'm not entirely sure.

I guess my problem is that I do not know where to begin. I've never attempted a journey such as this. I was exposed to some aspects of Christianity as a young child, but not by my family. I even own a Bible given to me on my eleventh birthday by a passing missionary woman. Inscribed inside is the date on which I prayed for Jesus to save me, but I no longer remember that day.

Do you have any advice for a person just beginning her journey to find God after twenty-three years of denial?

Reply: My heart goes out to you. You say you're not entirely sure what you're afraid of; well, I can tell you what most of us humans are afraid of when we come to the point that you've reached. We fear that the search will turn up empty, that there won't be any meaning after all. At the same time, we fear that the search *won't* turn up empty, because in that case the meaning must be God's; we aren't at liberty to make it up. Something in us would rather go on failing at being God than have God succeed at it.

Given that something, it is a miracle of grace that we can search for Him at all. You're experiencing that miracle now. Despite the fear of not finding God, despite the equally terrible fear of finding Him, you are searching for Him anyway. It is He who made this possible.

Here is my advice. The three counsels that follow are intended to be followed all at once—not one today, another in a week, and another in six months. They work together.

First, pray. Pray in the name of Christ, who is the revelation of God Himself in person, even though you don't yet know Him, and do so with all your heart. This is not what you prayed on your eleventh birthday with the missionary lady. The purpose of your prayer is to ask Him to lead you, by His own ways, into all His truth. Ask Him every day. I know you don't yet know whether anyone is listening. That's all right. You can pray to God, "I don't know if You're real, but if You are, You can have me. Just show me, because I can't tell." That's what I prayed when I was where you are. For months it seemed that nothing happened, but that was only because He had to clean so much out of my ears before I could hear Him.

Second, start living as though you were a Christian. You will often fail; so do we all. That's why we need Him. Remember that when we disobey Him, He doesn't stop speaking to us, but our ability to hear Him diminishes. It works the other way too. The more we obey, the better we hear.

Third, find the best church you can, worship as fully as you can, and learn everything about Christ that you can. The temptation is to think,

First I'll figure out what it means to be a lamb, then I'll go find the flock. No, for it's only in the flock that we learn what it means to be a lamb. You will need God's help to find a good church, but there is a practical side to it too. I've written about what to look for and avoid in *How to Stay Christian in College.*

When you are ready, arrange to be baptized, and follow Christ forever.

Don't lose heart. Remember, the fact that you are restless is a sign that He is calling your name. He loves us more than we love ourselves. He searches for us long before we search for Him. He never stops. And He is more wonderful than you can imagine.

Peace be with you,
Professor Theophilus

HOME FOR CHRISTMAS

Dear Professor Theophilus:

Everyone in my family except me is an atheist. At Christmastime, they deck the house out in Christmas stuff and play Christmas carols round-the-clock — but at the same time, they make a point of mocking Jesus and His followers! Back in high school, my decision to become a Christian provoked such serious arguments with my father and stepmother that I'm on don't-talk-about-faith terms with them. Even at other times of year the situation can be difficult. Once, when my stepsister saw a bumper sticker that said "Jesus loves you," she exclaimed that she hated the driver for it. But it gets worse when I'm home for the holidays.

I love my family and it hurts me to hear them talk like this. Please, give me some idea of how to speak for Jesus in such a way that they won't mock what I say and shut me out! I'd love to be able to take a stand without seeming obnoxious or self-righteous, but I know that if I do they'll get angry, and I'm afraid I won't be able to handle the situation gracefully.

Reply: I sympathize, and here is how I advise. Be charitable, humble, grateful, and forbearing toward your family; rejoice in their good qualities, and show your appreciation for them; be actively helpful by doing things like running errands and washing all the dishes without being asked; go on about your Christian business, like worshipping at church on Sunday and on Christmas Eve, without calling attention to yourself; try *not* to try to force your family to be what they aren't; and one more. The last one is to pray for your family. Do it without ceasing. Leave it to God Himself to decide how to answer your prayers.

I know you want to do something more. You want to hurry God. You want to "take a stand." My heart goes out to you. But believe me, practicing love toward your family *is* taking a stand. They know you're a Christian; it isn't necessary to talk Christ if they aren't yet ready to hear Christ. If they grow irritated with you even for loving them, love them even more.

By the way, if they want to sing Christmas carols, join them! Why not? You might ask them some year *why* they sing them, but don't fret about the fact that they don't believe them. There may be more going on in their hearts than you think. Considering how angrily they fight against Jesus, perhaps they are feeling His pull. Would you rather that they be indifferent? Who knows what the Holy Spirit can do? You may all end up saints. Have a blessed Advent and a merry Christmas.

Peace be with you,
Professor Theophilus

NOTES

1. Pre-Modern Studies.
2. "It seemed good to me also, having followed all things closely for some time past, to write an orderly account for you, most excellent Theophilus" (Luke 1:3). Unless otherwise specified, all biblical passages are from the Revised Standard Version.
3. Formerly at www.boundless.org, now at www.TrueU.org.
4. This is the opening sentence of John Paul II, *Fides et Ratio* ("Faith and Reason").
5. Lactantius, *The Divine Institutes*, Bk. 5, Chap. 20. You can look up the passage at http://www.ccel.org/fathers.html or at http://www.newadvent.org/fathers/ . These translations are in the public domain.
6. If you find this answer helpful, check out "Workaholic, Friendaphobic" in "College Relationships Letters."
7. 1 Thessalonians 5:17.
8. Matthew 22:37.
9. Proverbs 1:7.
10. Proverbs 3:19-20.
11. Proverbs 8:32-33,35-36.
12. John 1:1-4.
13. See "The Comeback Sin" in "Fleeing Toward God Stuff."
14. The conversation turned out to take a little longer. You can read it in *Ask Me Anything 1* under the title "Sex at the Edge of Night."
15. Matthew 11:28-30.
16. 1 Corinthians 10:13.
17. In the answers to other letters, and in another book, *How to Stay Christian in College*, Chap. 8.
18. Matthew 4:7.
19. St. Augustine of Hippo, *Confessions*, 2d ed., Bk. 1, Chap. 1, trans. by F. J. Sheed, ed. by Michael P. Foley (Indianapolis: Hackett Publishing Co., 2006), 3.
20. G. K. Chesterton, *The Penguin Complete Father Brown* (New York: Penguin Books, 1981), 110.
21. James 2:19.

22. C. S. Lewis, *Mere Christianity* (New York: Macmillan, 1952), 52-53.

23. See, for example, the stanza of "O Come, O Come, Emmanuel," which runs, "O come, Desire of nations, bind / in one the hearts of all mankind; / bid thou our sad divisions cease, / and be thyself our King of Peace." The image comes from Haggai 2:7, in the Old Testament, though it is not equally clear in all translations.

24. Mark 9:24.

25. Matthew 11:28.

26. John 3:16.

27. 1 Timothy 1:15.

28. 1 John 2:1-2.

29. St. Augustine of Hippo, *Sermons on the Liturgical Seasons*, trans. by Sr. Mary Sarah Muldowney, R.S.M., Vol. 38 in The Fathers of the Church, ed. Roy Joseph Deferrari (New York: Fathers of the Church, Inc., 1959), 28.

30. Ecclesiastes 1:8.

31. Romans 15:4.

32. Romans 8:19-20 — but keep reading.

33. Romans 8:22-23.

34. Romans 8:26.

35. 2 Corinthians 12:9.

36. Proverbs 15:22.

37. Cited previously.

38. Romans 1:18-20.

39. John 10:3-4,27.

40. John 10:16.

41. Matthew 7:13-14.

42. St. Augustine of Hippo, *Confessions* (cited previously), Bk. 8, Chap. 7.

43. "Why I Am Not an Atheist," in Norman L. Geisler and Paul K. Hoffman, eds., *Why I Am a Christian: Leading Thinkers Explain Why They Believe* (Grand Rapids: Baker Books, 2001), 49-61.

44. If you want to read the article, plug the title into the search engine of your browser.

ABOUT THE AUTHOR

J. BUDZISZEWSKI (Boojee-shef-skee) is the author of numerous books, including the best-selling *How to Stay Christian in College*. A professor of government and philosophy at the University of Texas, Dr. Budziszewski lives in Austin, Texas, with his wife, Sandra.

"TH1NK for Yourself"
Other great titles from TH1NK

Own Your Faith

Mark Tabb
ISBN-13: 978-1-60006-097-7
ISBN-10: 1-60006-097-8

How can you learn to think for yourself and make your faith your own—not the faith of your parents, youth leaders, or pastor? This insightful yet humorous guide will lead you through the process of grappling with and living out your convictions in a postmodern world.

How to Stay Christian in College

J. Budziszewski
ISBN-13: 978-1-57683-510-4
ISBN-10: 1-57683-510-3

Warning: College can be hazardous to your spiritual health. Even if you're going to a "Christian" college, there's no guarantee you won't face challenges to your faith. So how *do* you stay Christian in college?

The Message//REMIX Solo

Eugene H. Peterson
ISBN-13: 978-1-60006-105-9
ISBN-10: 1-60006-105-2

This innovative devotional is designed to change how you interact with God's Word. *The Message Remix: Solo* revolves around lectio divina, or "divine reading," an ancient approach to exploring Scripture updated for today's students

To order copies, visit your local Christian bookstore,
call NavPress at 1-800-366-7788, or log on to www.navpress.com.

To locate a Christian bookstore near you, call 1-800-991-7747.